Contents

Landlord and Tenant:
the new regime and its pitfalls

A critical guide to the
Landlord and Tenant (Covenants) Act 1995

MARTIN BOXER

SOLICITOR

Cavendish
Publishing
Limited

First published in Great Britain 1996 by Cavendish Publishing Limited, The Glass House, Wharton Street, London WC1X 9PX.

Telephone: 0171-278 8000   Facsimile: 0171-278 8080

Boxer, M
Landlord and Tenant: the new regime and its pitfalls
I.Landlord and tenant – England
I.Title
344.2'06434

ISBN 1 85941 283 1

Printed and bound in Great Britain

Preface

The idea that led to this book emanated from a long-standing professional acquaintance of the author, who, very soon after the Landlord and Tenant (Covenants) Act 1995 came onto the statute book, buttonholed him at a reception to remonstrate with him at its perceived iniquities. Taken aback at the force of this re-action, the author took himself off to HM Stationary Office in Holborn to purchase a copy of the Act, whereupon he plucked up the courage to immerse himself in its contents.

The author found himself intrigued by the revolutionary nature of the legislation, at least in terms of the law of landlord and tenant, but non-plussed by his acquaintance's fulminations against the perpetrators of the new Act. Emboldened by the latter's strictures that he was just the man to explain to the wider world the basics of the changes, having spent for better or worse over thirty years battling away at the coalface dealing with the practical consequences of the subject, he prepared an outline of the Act's main provisions with a view to publication at or shortly after the Act becoming effective.

However, it did not take the author long to see the error of his ways and the thrust of his colleague's initial complaints.

The Landlord and Tenant (Covenants) Act 1995 does, indeed, fundamentally alter the relationship between these two concepts but leaves unanswered, in some cases very obviously deliberately, a whole series of questions emanating from the structures it sets up as additions to, or replacements for, a regime itself created over 70 years ago.

The more the author delved into the mysteries of the new legislation the more obvious it became to him that a mere understanding of its basic principles could leave any person concerned with a lease or tenancy dangerously exposed to problems of which he or she could well be oblivious. Contact with any number of the leading practitioners in this field fortified the author in this view and led him to the conclusion that his offering on the subject, at some risk to his sanity, should be extended so as to concentrate on also highlighting some of the problems lying in wait for the unwary.

To do this, the author relied on help from a large number of sources too numerous to list here. However, he must refer to the following who unstintingly gave of their valuable time and substantial expertise in an effort to keep him on the straight and narrow.

Nick Taggart of Counsel (with an honourable mention to the Senior Clerk at 4 Breams Buildings for his forebearance)

Roger Sutcliffe and Gill Briant of Denton Hall

and Geoffrey Silman of Nathan, Silman.

It is hoped that they all find the final result of the author's labours to have been worth the effort they put in and that it will contribute in some small way to enlightening the wider world to an area of the law which has ramifications for everybody involved in the property world.

Introduction

The overriding purpose behind this guide is to provide the necessary ammunition to deal with the consequences in the real world of what is probably the most fundamental change to the law in England and Wales concerning the relationship between landlords and tenants for over 70 years – certainly, in the commercial world, since the legislation to give business tenants security of tenure rights was introduced in 1954. There are numerous explanations of what the Act contains but it is hoped that this guide will be sufficiently 'user-friendly' to be of practical benefit to all who read it. To this end, some of the more technical consequences of the Act's introduction have been omitted from this guide; instead the reader will find highlighted Rules to be borne in mind so as to ensure that the vitally important practical consequences and potential pitfalls of the Act are not forgotten.

The purpose behind the legislation is to end the perceived iniquities of 'privity of contract', a basic rule of landlord and tenant since time immemorial which has, in effect, bound the original tenant to the obligations it entered into on the grant of the tenancy for the length of its term irrespective of whether it remained the tenant in possession, actually paying the rent and otherwise taking responsibility for those obligations. Long perceived by academics, at least, as inequitable, the commercial world only started to take serious notice during the last recession when, not unnaturally, landlords, faced with impecunious tenants, looked round for someone else to provide the income they had budgeted to receive from their property.

The nation's retailers were particularly upset at being hounded to discharge all sorts of obligations they had long forgotten about and their trade association, the British Retail Consortium, lobbied long and hard (and ultimately successfully) to persuade Parliament that the time had come to remove the 'iniquitous' rule from the system. However, their opposite numbers looking after the interests of the property industry, the British Property Federation, were equally determined to ensure that, at the very least, the baby did not go out with the bathwater. When it was pointed out that in Scotland no great trauma was caused by the rule not being enforced north of the border, the BPF could fairly point out that neither were there security of tenure rights for business tenants when their lease expired. At least in Scotland you knew you could usually say goodbye to your tenant if you wanted to find another one.

The upshot was, of course, in the great British tradition; a compromise. In what appears a highly unusual arrangement, the two bodies and their advisers entered into a negotiation as to the terms of the new Bill, the parties being 'lent' a parliamentary draftsman for the purpose. As their advisers included highly skilled and experienced property lawyers, well versed in the problems of interfacing technical issues with the real world, it is not surprising that they have come up with a set of innovative solutions to the problem of resolving the opposing positions in an equitable and balanced fashion.

However, it remains to be seen whether they have successfully coped with one aspect of the real world probably outside their normal experience, namely the pressures of meeting parliamentary deadlines. To meet the window of opportunity for turning the Bill into an Act, it seems that some of the tidying up of the drafting had to be curtailed; certainly, there are any number of loose ends which will need to be carefully watched and are likely to entice those brave enough to risk litigation. That there will be litigation on how the Act is to be interpreted is certain. This guide will endeavour to point out some of the apparent uncertainties, and others will assuredly manifest themselves as the mechanisms of the Act are implemented.

The start date for the purposes of the Act was 1 January 1996. This date, referred to from now on as 'the start date', is of vital importance since the abolition of the privity of contract rule is not retrospective, ie if a tenancy was granted for the purposes of the Act before the start date – an 'old' lease as this guide calls it – in the main, the old law applies but with three significant retrospective changes, all brought in by the Act but none changing the basic privity of contract rule. Most (but not all) tenancies granted from the start date – 'new tenancies' as the Act calls them – will have the whole Act applying to them, including, therefore the parts applying to old leases as well.

Notice that not all tenancies granted after the start date are new tenancies. If the landlord is fortunate enough to have or have brought about a situation before the start date where its tenant had been signed up to an agreement, option or pre-emption right or, by that date, a court order had been obtained, pursuant to any of which a tenancy is granted after that date, it is still an old lease for the purposes of the Act. There is at least one more situation where a lease granted after the start date is nevertheless an old lease, but more of that later.

> **Rule 1: from the point of view of all sides, it is undoubtedly good practice to insert in the body of the lease a statement as to whether, for the purposes of the Act, it is an old lease or a new tenancy. Also, proposed assignees ought to ensure that, notwithstanding the above, all necessary enquiries have been made to check in specific terms that the lease has been correctly defined by asking about court orders etc.**

This guide assumes that the terms of an old lease had been settled before the start up date and, for our purposes, are immutable. In fact, there is, of course, nothing to stop the parties agreeing to vary them to accommodate changes brought in by the Act but, beware, the existing law can hurt you when you may not be expecting it and one of the Act's changes concerns the consequences that can flow from such variations.

Before turning to where old leases now stand, it must be remembered that, save in the circumstances mentioned later, the Act applies just as much to residential and agricultural tenancies as it does to business ones; for a start the property investment industry was a good deal more exercised about the effect of the abolition of the privity of contract rule on commercial property where covenant strength has traditionally played such a significant part in assessing value. The Act even expressly provides that the Crown will be bound by it. The only covenants in tenancies not touched at all by the Act relate to such matters as repayment of proceeds on early disposal of a residential property acquired under the right to buy legislation etc.

Before we begin in earnest, some more points to bear in mind on terminology:

(1) The word 'covenants' in the Act and, therefore, also in this guide, has a far wider meaning than commonly understood. It extends, therefore, beyond an obligation expressed as a covenant in a lease to include any 'term, condition and obligation' (but not a right of re-entry), whether in the tenancy document itself or in any agreement collateral to that tenancy, whether made before or after its creation (eg agreement for lease, side letter, rent deposit agreement, related agreement with a management company, licence under the tenancy provisions, deed of variation).

(2) The use of the words 'tenancy' and 'lease' are fully interchangeable for the purposes of this guide.

(3) Any statement in this guide concerning the Act's contents is accompanied by a reference to the commensurate section of the Act which is set out in full as Appendix I.

(4) The party with the reversion and their predecessors and successors and those deriving title through the reversion have been made inanimate in this guide, ie the landlord is an 'it', whilst those deriving their interest through the term granted by the respective tenancy or lease are assumed to be animate, ie the tenant is a 'he'. No slur is intended to landlords and their representatives by so doing, nor to women who may feel equally aggrieved the tenant is not a 'she'!

Part I: Old leases

It is not the purpose of this guide to provide a dissertation on the old law and practice concerning tenants' liability. However, some comments are needed, if only so that the changes the Act introduces can be more readily taken on board.

(1) It has long been accepted practice that an assignee or any guarantor or surety he offers will be required by the landlord, unless it can be ignored, to provide a direct covenant to be responsible for the tenants' obligations during the remainder of the lease term, thus putting the assignee and any sureties he may have on all fours with the original tenant.

> **Rule 2: there is no reason why a landlord should not continue to insist on a direct covenant when its tenant wants to assign an old lease, although it must always have regard to the restrictions dealt with below that the Act now imposes on recovery from that tenant (and any predecessors) once he has assigned.**

(2) It follows from the above that, when the current tenant of an old lease defaults, a prudent landlord who has taken appropriate direct covenants on an assignment can, subject to the one now important caveat which we will come to, choose to pursue most claims against all or any of the original tenant, intermediate assignees and all sureties, including any guaranteeing the current tenant. Indeed, the House of Lords has just decided in *Hardcastle Ltd v Barbara Attenborough Associates Ltd* [1996] 1 All ER 737 that disclaimer of the lease in question after the insolvency of the current tenant will no longer of itself cause any surety of the tenant's obligations to be released, a change in the interpretation of statute law as it had stood previously for over 90 years. Except when it came to a disclaimer, none of those listed above, however, had the right, in common or statute law, as a consequence of meeting such claims, to require back possession of the property, even if the lease were forfeited. That, as we shall see, has also now changed.

Thus, for example, an earlier tenant may well remain liable to the landlord for the cost of dilapidations even though he had paid a reverse premium to his assignee at the time of assignment in respect of the then lack of repair. This happens because, whilst strictly, his assignee is not liable to the landlord for breaches of covenant committed by a prior tenant, where the breach 'touches and concerns' the premises demised, as when there has been a failure to repair, the assignee becomes liable even though he was not responsible for the original breach.

(3) Before the Act was passed, even if lease obligations were materially altered between the landlord and its then tenant by their agreeing, say, a wider permitted user for the tenant in return for an increase in rent, the law was that the original tenant and the intermediate tenants who gave direct covenants remained liable for that increase. That is no longer the case, not only because of statutory change introduced by the Act but also because of changes to the common law introduced by the Court of Appeal, as will be amplified below.

Further, in reality, by drafting direct guarantee covenants carefully, it was thought that sureties could be placed in the same position as the tenant they were acting as surety for rather than being released when a material change to the tenant's obligations was made without their consent. Recent court decisions, nothing to do with the Act, have made it essential to check again the effectiveness of such provisions although, in any case, the relevant changes introduced by the Act as they affect old leases will apply equally to sureties as to the tenants they guarantee.

The Act does not, however, alter the basic legal principle that a variation deemed to constitute a surrender and re-grant of the lease, recently reiterated by the Court of Appeal as likely to happen only when the lease's term is lengthened or the premises demised by the lease are increased, will always release the earlier tenants as well as all sureties, irrespective of the parties' intentions.

> **Rule 3: if the lease before such a variation had been an old lease, a change of the latter type will metamorphose it into a new tenancy for the purpose of the Act. Landlords should bear this in mind before they agree such variations if they wish to preserve the ability to use the privity of contract rule at all.**

The Act's three main provisions affecting old leases

NB – they also affect new tenancies

Restrictions on recovery of arrears

This provision is the most important as far as old leases are concerned.

Anybody concerned with the management of commercial or residential property must be fully conversant with it and its consequences.

A defence is given by the Act (s 17) to *former tenants* (including the original tenant) *and their guarantors* against any claim under a lease which comes within the definition of 'fixed charge' in the Act. Such a party will *not be liable* for sums which come within the definition unless notice in a prescribed form is given 'within the period of six months beginning with the date when the charge becomes due' (s 17(2)). This begs the question of whether the landlord can only start its proceedings after its notice has been served since that is what is required to trigger the liability into existence. Claims recoverable in respect of matters not deemed to be 'fixed charges' can be pursued without such prior notice in the same way as previously.

For a surety to get the benefit of this protection it *must* be guaranteeing a former tenant, not the actual tenant in possession (s 17(3)).

What does 'fixed charge' mean?

It encompasses all rent, all relevant service charges, the payment of a 'liquidated sum' due from the tenant following his failure to comply with any of his covenants and any appropriate interest and costs (s 17(6)).

'Rent'

Any obligation to pay rent, however the amount is calculated, is covered. Thus, a landlord may well have provided for the payment of at least service charge, insurance premium and interest to be reserved as 'rent', which means such payments are 'fixed charges' for this purpose. How much farther a landlord may have used the word 'rent' to cover whatever other monies will or might become due from the tenant, will need to be reviewed in each case but, in theory, it can cover everything, so as to give the recipient of a claim the chance to avoid needing to argue over the other definitions used for assessing what is and is not a 'fixed charge'.

'Service charge'

This is defined by reference to any sum which is payable, either directly or indirectly, for services, repairs, maintenance or insurance or in relation to the landlord's costs of management. Assuming that it is not clearly within the definition of 'rent' in any case, recipients of claims under the new procedure may well find the above definition sufficiently wide to be able to cover certain items of charge often seen in today's service charge but whose inclusion can be controversial, eg the cost of publicity for and marketing of shopping centres. Are they an amount '... payable directly or indirectly for services'?

'Liquidated sum'

There is some guidance as to what this means but not a lot. Until and unless a modern court of law gets to grips with this definition, the best view seems to be that the sum due has to be ascertained or ascertainable under the covenants of the tenant to the landlord 'as a mere matter of arithmetic'.

On this basis, it does not include, say, claims for breach of the tenant's repairing covenant or the alienation provisions since they are, at least initially, unliquidated claims but query whether a notice should be given after a liquidated sum has been determined in consequence of such a breach. The Act states that the tenant must be obliged to pay a liquidated sum '*in the event* of a failure to comply' so perhaps not. However, a landlord may be loath to take the risk.

NB The use of the word 'fixed' in the definition is somewhat misleading in so far as the sum claimed can vary, as mentioned below.

> **Rule 4: be very careful when considering whether, as well as when, a 'fixed charge' has become due. A tenant, in particular, should always check to see whether the amount claimed can properly be called such, particularly bearing in mind that he may have more than one option open to him in arguing that it is. If he can claim the demand is for a 'fixed charge', the next step is to get his diary out to see if the six-month time limit has expired. If that does not work, he can still read on to see whether the landlord has complied with the requisite procedural steps.**
>
> **If the landlord is not clear whether its claim is for a 'fixed charge' or not, it is better to be cautious and assume the former.**

What does the landlord (including for this purpose any person with a right to enforce payment eg a receiver or mortgagee in possession (s 17(6)) have to do to protect its position?

1 Pre-start date arrears

Arrears due before the start date of 1 January 1996, but where no relevant proceedings have yet been begun against the relevant former tenant (**NB**: action against his guarantor does not count), are treated as becoming due on that date, ie the six-month clock for the default notice to be served then starts ticking. Therefore, a landlord must have served its notice on or before *30 June 1996* to avoid being stymied.

Beware one thing, however. Any tenant or guarantor who pays up following a default notice is entitled to require the grant to him of an overriding lease, of which more below, and a landlord needs to balance this against the obvious desire to protect to the maximum its ability to recover outstanding debt.

2 All other arrears

The six months runs from when the fixed charge becomes due. The Act makes it mandatory that the notice is *served* by the end of that period, ie time is of the essence.

Therefore, remember the clock starts ticking from when the payment becomes due (s 17(2)). It seems a landlord cannot agree instalment payments in return for its opposite number waiving the six-month rule, especially if it wants to preserve rights in respect of the same claim against others.

Especially remember, when considering quarter day rests, that the periods between March and September and June and December quarter days exceed six months!

Rule 5: landlords must ensure their records and procedures are tight enough to pick up all relevant fixed charges and appropriate deadlines for their payment but having regard to the perceived risk of the recipient wanting an overriding lease after payment. There is no second chance so, if you get it wrong, you may need to check the negligence or redundancy policy! Don't forget the tenant's undertenants who might well have given you direct covenants if your consent was needed to the underlease. They are not covered by the Act and they might save you a lot of trouble.

Former tenants and their sureties just need to keep their heads down but get their act together quickly if they do get a notice, and do not forget to check for any variation to the lease terms which may also get them off the hook or, at least, reduce their liability. Also they should check to ensure the lease has not been surrendered or forfeited, maybe unwittingly. It is not unknown for a site inspection to reveal an unknown party in occupation and open the way for a surrender to be capable of being evidenced to a court's satisfaction.

What form does the notice have to take and how is it served?

To be effective, the default notice must be in the form set out by the Lord Chancellor in regulations which came into effect on the start up date (see Form 1 to Schedule of the Landlord (Covenants) Act 1995 (Notices) Regulations 1995 – p 107 of Appendix II), or in a form 'substantially to the same effect' (s 27(4)) but, in any event, to include the following:

(1)   the fixed charge then due;

(2)   the amount in respect of it intended to be recovered;

(3)   the basis of calculating any interest;

(4)   the possibility that liability for a greater sum may be subsequently determined (if the landlord wishes to retain the statutory right referred to below to recover a larger amount than originally specified); and

(5)   an explanation of the significance of the notice.

Rule 6: the landlord needs to ensure that the prescribed form of the default notice is carefully followed since this is another case where it will not get another chance if it gets it wrong, unless it discovers its error in time to serve another before the six months run out; the Act does not seem to bar this. Otherwise, it must hope the mistake is found to be sufficiently trivial not to matter; initially, at least, this may be a recipe for litigation.

The Act states that the standard rules on service relating to tenancies shall apply (s 27(5)) ie a written notice is required served either personally or (preferably) by recorded delivery or by registered post to the recipient's last known place of abode or, where applicable, to his principal office, including in this respect, in the case of a company, its registered office.

> **Rule 7: as mentioned in Rule 5, a landlord, before it comes up against its deadline, should ensure that it has an address for service for its old tenants and sureties.**

What does a landlord do after its initial default notice when it finds it is owed more money than it then specified in respect of the same fixed charge, eg in the case of a pending rent review or an interim service charge payment?

As indicated above, *only* provided it advised the recipient in the original notice of the possibility that liability for a greater amount might be determined, the landlord on such determination has the chance, by serving another notice in the prescribed form *within three months* of the determination, to increase the limit of recovery to the greater amount to which the new notice must specify his liability now amounts (plus any interest) (s 17(4) and see Form 2 of Appendix II, p 110).

One problem not solved by the legislation is whether you can serve more than one follow-up notice for each fixed-charge debt. The legislation does not seem to envisage more than one 'subsequent determination', and hence further notice, as required to cover increases in the fixed-charge debt, but is this necessarily correct? Hence the next question.

What amounts to 'determination' for the above purposes?

A good question, to which there is no clear answer in the absence of any definition in the Act. In most cases, the answer may appear clear but fertile legal minds can, no doubt, think of examples when it is not, eg when is a rent review 'determined' for this purpose?

> **Rule 8: whenever there is uncertainty, the only prudent action the landlord can take is to serve a default notice for each assumed determination on the basis that one at least will be held to be effective. This assumes, of course, that it has satisfied itself on the downside of the recipient paying but also wanting his overriding lease.**

One final thought before passing on. The Act seems to assume that a good notice properly served makes the recipient liable to pay the amount specified. Will the courts, therefore, assume that the landlord can automatically exercise all its remedies for recovery of the debt against the tenant? The answer is surely not. As the law presently stands, it is difficult to see how, by claiming payment of monies due under a lease in accordance with the wording prescribed for the default notice, the landlord cannot have done other than waive any right to go for forfeiture of that lease due to that breach, a right which depends on it doing nothing which recognises the lease's continued existence.

The claimant's right to an overriding lease

This is another of the Act's innovations which is likely to have wide implications. It endeavours to deal with the earlier widely perceived weakness in the law which left a previous tenant and/or surety responsible for all tenancy debts and responsibilities but without any control over that tenancy unless able to obtain a vesting order once the current tenant's trustee in bankruptcy or liquidator had disclaimed the lease.

Only, however, a claimant (as he is called in the Act – (s 19(1))) who has paid up *in full (including interest)* under a default notice of the type outlined above can claim the benefit. He does this by requesting the landlord to grant him an overriding lease of the relevant premises which, provided there is compliance with the Act, the landlord must complete (s 19(1)).

In practice, both sides, the landlord and the claimant, have the option of deciding whether they want to go down this route. The landlord does not have to serve the default notice on the claimant in the first place and there is no obligation on the claimant to take up the new lease after fully discharging the terms of the default notice.

The overriding lease is intended to put the claimant in the position of the landlord's tenant instead of the errant tenant whose breach of his lease caused the new lease to be created in the first place: the latter should, as a result, become the claimant's tenant.

As the errant tenant's new landlord, the claimant, assuming that it is still facing problems from breaches of covenant, but not (save as mentioned later in this paragraph) the breach which led to the new lease being granted, essentially has three options. It may, if, for a start, not caught by the six-month rule, be able to commence the whole process again against other appropriate previous tenants and/or sureties through the default notice procedure; it might see if it can enforce any worthwhile indemnity covenants it has lawfully the benefit of through its earlier involvement with the old lease (which could, in practice, well include recovery of the original debt); or it may decide to go for forfeiture or re-entry, if it has a re-entry clause in the old lease, to give it possession against the current tenant.

However, as this guide will endeavour to show, there are a number of hidden snags for both sides in pursuing their respective paths and they should both weigh up very carefully the implications before proceeding.

One not so hidden snag which the landlord should always be eminently capable of dealing with needs to be reiterated at this juncture. It must consider all its options and the inherent risks and benefits before firing off default notices against its previous tenants and their sureties, bearing in mind, of course, its time deadline as, once it has done so, it does to a large extent, albeit not entirely, lose control of events.

Rule 9: landlords should be particularly wary of serving default notices on weak tenants or those they are not so keen to see occupying their property. If they are especially concerned, they might prefer going for forfeiture, remembering the earlier comment as to the likelihood of a default notice waiving that right in relation to that breach.

It would be good estate management for them not to lose track of what previous tenants and sureties have been doing so that they can exercise their commercial judgment with as much information as possible before them.

Has the Act left parties unprotected by restricting the benefits of taking up an overriding lease to a claimant discharging his default notice?

Yes, certainly, in one respect, for tenants; and, very likely, in another respect, for landlords.

(1) As indicated earlier, it has always been (and can remain with old leases) normal procedure on an assignment for the assignee and any surety it offers to indemnify the assignor against any subsequent breach. Then, if the landlord, on a requisite breach occurring, serves its default notice on the assignor who pays and, thus, asks for its overriding lease, there is, as we have seen above, nothing to stop the assignor suing his assignee (or the latter, surety) and recovering the money. The recipient of the writ, even though himself a former tenant (or his surety) and not the current tenant, has no right to insist on being granted an overriding lease if and when he pays!

> **Rule 10: when you take an assignment of an old lease and are asked for the indemnity, you should insist on a clause in the contract requiring the assignor (and its surety?) paying up on receipt of a default notice, to take up the overriding lease and assign it on, following your having reimbursed him the debt in accordance with the indemnity.**

(2) The Act states that the claimant entitled to the overriding lease is '*any person*' who makes full payment of the amount demanded of him through the default notice procedure (s 19(1)). The Act also provides that the notice should be served on an appropriate 'person' which it thereafter calls 'the former tenant' (s 17(1)).

Thus, it would seem, on the face of it, perfectly legitimate for one party to call for a lease in response to a default notice even though there were others who were tenants of the lease with him, say, members of the same family taking up a residential lease or members of a partnership taking an office, all of whom may have been served with a notice. If so, there seems nothing to stop such joint tenants putting up just one of their number to make full payment of the debt so as to be entitled to take up the lease as the claimant, even though he may offer the weakest covenant to the landlord.

The Act offers no specific guidance on the point and you are left to rely for any further help on the statement that, 'where two or more persons jointly constitute ... the tenant ... any reference ... to the tenant is a reference to both or all of the persons who jointly constitute the tenant' (s 28(4)). Whereas that may well be enough, unfortunately for the landlord, to make it requisite in order to be binding for a default notice to be served on all the joint tenants due to the use of the terminology 'former tenant' in this context (s 17(1)), it is difficult, but not impossible, to see that phrase as being capable of being extended to cover the 'person' who is entitled to have the new lease. He is not defined as a 'tenant' of any description but expressly as 'the claimant' (s 19(1)).

> **Rule 11: where there is a situation that the landlord is looking to serve default notices on former joint tenants, the parties must assume, pending any guidance from the courts, that it has to serve a default notice or default notices on all of them to make the process effective but then has no control over which of them it becomes required to grant the overriding lease to. However, both sides should be aware of Rule 15!**

What has the claimant got to do to get his overriding lease, and can either he or his potential landlord change their mind?

(1) He has to make a written request of the landlord, specifying the payment which he claims entitles him to the lease (s 19(5)(a)). There is no other requirement as to the form of the notice and the request may be sent by post (s 19(10)) where use of registered post or recorded delivery is to be recommended. However, to ensure it binds a purchaser of the landlord's reversion, it should be protected by notice or a caution at the Land Registry or, in the case of unregistered land, by registration of an estate contract at the Land Charges Registry (s 20(6)).

(2) There cannot be two valid requests for an overriding lease outstanding at the same time (s 19(7)(b)) and, whilst the general rule is that the first to apply gets it, there are also rules governing priority if, by some chance, two claimants put in requests on the same day – see s 19(8).

(3) For the request to be effective, it must be made *within 12 months*, starting from the date the claimant made the qualifying payment (s 19(5)(b)).

> **Rule 12: whilst 12 months should in any case be sufficient for a claimant to decide whether it wants the overriding lease, the use of the word 'must' in the Act, it is prudent to assume, implies an intent again to make time of the essence. No claimant should allow himself to be put in a position where he has to test this proposition and he must particularly want to bear in mind para (5) below.**

(4) Subject to the above, the landlord must complete the lease within 'a reasonable time' (s 19(6)(a)); whatever that means, it needs to be borne in mind that the landlord will be in breach of a statutory duty if it does not and can be sued in tort (s 20(3)). To this end, the Act provides that the lease shall be deemed authorised by any mortgagee of the landlord's interest and binding on it (s 20(4)). However, the Act does state that a mortgagee entitled to the deeds shall be sent the counterpart within one month of completion (s 20(4)(I)).

Surprisingly, the situation where the landlord is contractually obliged to obtain consent from a superior landlord is not adequately made clear at all in the Act. It appears only to cover absolving the claimant from any breach of covenants in the overriding lease against subletting caused by the continuing existence of the old lease (s 20(5)(b)). If so, the landlord may be in the difficult position of being accused of being in breach of its contractual obligations to its landlord whilst being obliged to continue with the grant of the overriding lease. In the final resort, though, it should remember the (on the face of it) stringent anti-avoidance provisions of the Act (see s 25 and from page 69 below) and might well wish to rely on them as supporting it against the superior landlord if the claimant insists on his new lease.

Rule 13: although is reasonable to assume from the above that, in the event of conflict, the landlord's statutory obligation will be held to override the contractual with regard to a mortgagee, with no consequential adverse consequences to it, a cautious landlord might at least want to notify its mortgagee of what is going on, especially in the light of what is said below regarding costs. So far as where it stands where consent from a superior landlord is stated to be necessary, it must be prudent to notify the latter at the earliest opportunity of the position, to give the maximum time for any conflicts to be resolved.

Rule 14: a mortgagee, if properly advised, may well be able to require to have varied the mortgage deed or other form of lending instrument with regard to the ability of the landlord to issue default notices without its consent. Certainly, all new mortgages should be altered accordingly and superior landlords may well want to consider their position, if and when they get the chance.

(5) There is an apparent loophole in the Act which appears to allow a landlord, if it plays its cards right, to avoid having to grant a claimant an overriding lease even though he has discharged the claimed debt and has validly exercised his right to be granted the lease.

The scenario is as follows:

(a) The landlord serves its default notice on the former tenant in the prescribed form which states that it 'intends to recover from you' the claimed amount (see Form 1 Appendix II, p 101). In doing so, remember that it is likely to have waived the relevant breach of covenant leading to the claim.

(b)   The former tenant pays the claim and asks for his overriding lease in the appropriate way.

(c)   Whilst the landlord is not yet in breach of its obligation to be ready to complete the new lease within a reasonable period, another breach of the tenants' covenants in the extant lease occurs which entitles afresh the landlord to forfeit the same or re-enter. The landlord has been prudent and has not taken such action in relation to the original breach after it served the default notice so as to give the claimant the opportunity to allege waiver by virtue of the notice's wording.

(d)   Without ado, the landlord now terminates (and keeps terminated) the extant lease through forfeiture or re-entry and refuses to then complete the overriding lease, citing the provision in the Act which specifically states that it 'shall not be under any obligation to grant an overriding lease … at a time when the [extant lease] has been determined' (s 19(7))!

Rule 15: one of the factors for the former tenant to bear in mind is to check the extant lease for upcoming possible breaches of tenant's covenant – say, the dates of future quarters' rent payments – so as to time its request for a new lease to avoid the landlord being given a chance to terminate the former before being obliged to grant the latter. Alternatively, it will have to take steps to try and ensure any such breach is rectified or otherwise the termination stopped. Query whether the courts might in due course give a claimant at least the right to obtain relief against forfeiture on appropriate terms?

The landlord will need to rely on the best advice available if it wants to try and avoid having to complete the overriding lease but may be particularly tempted if faced with the wrong joint tenant as claimant – remember Rule 11.

(6)   If the claimant, following receipt of the original lease duly executed from the landlord, fails to then deliver to the landlord the counterpart also executed, *and* fails to pay all the landlord's reasonable costs, the Act expressly states that the claimant cannot exercise any of the rights given to him by that lease, eg take forfeiture or possession proceedings against the errant tenant to get back occupation or relet (s 20(3)).

(7)   The claimant can withdraw in writing (but no set form) (s 19(9)(a)) his request for a new lease to the landlord at any time before completion whilst he is regarded as having abandoned the request if he fails to comply with a written request (again no set form) from the landlord to take all or any of the outstanding steps required of him within a reasonable period to be specified in the landlord's request (s 19(9)(b)). But he must remember that, in either case, he is still liable

for the landlord's reasonable costs to date (s 19(9)) although, whilst his request remains outstanding, no other claimant can insist on being granted by the landlord an overriding lease (s 19(7)(b)).

(8) When deciding whether or not to proceed with the request for a lease or to follow it through to completion, the former tenant should bear in mind that, as lessee, he will have to bear stamp duty and also Land Registry fees (if the lease is for 21 years or over) in the usual way on completion, as well as the landlord's reasonable costs.

(9) The fact that a landlord holds its interest in the property through an overriding lease does not in itself prevent there being a successful claim to another one in respect of that property from a different claimant who has paid up following receipt of a default notice (s 19(11)). Thus, there is no bar on the number of overriding leases but what is not allowed is for a claimant to insist on an overriding lease where his proposed landlord has already granted one which remains in force (s 19(7)(a)) or, as we have just seen, where there is an outstanding request for one yet to be withdrawn or abandoned (s 19(7)(b)).

(10) Just because the overriding lease is completed after the Act's start date does not of itself mean that it will be subject to the full terms of the Act as a new tenancy. *Whether it is or not is governed by the date of the extant tenancy only, ie the lease the breach of which led to the default notice* (see s 20(1)).

In the context of this part of this guide, therefore, all overriding leases created out of an old lease are themselves old leases.

What form does the overriding lease have to take and is it immutable?

(1) Yet one further hidden trap in the Act, this time for a putative claimant of business premises, lies in the reversionary period of up to but not exceeding *three* days that must be added to the term of the old extant lease to form the term of the overriding lease; it has to be less than *three* days to the extent that the landlord's own reversionary interest does not stretch that far (s 19(2)(a)).

Of course, business tenants, when their contractual term ceases, have rights to a new lease under the 1954 legislation which are based on such a tenant being in occupation of the relevant demise for that purpose. The problem is that a reversion of three days, on any realistic basis, is insufficient time of itself for the claimant, once landlord of the old lease, to have a chance of obtaining possession and running a business as this is interpreted for the purposes of the Landlord and Tenant Act 1954.

This problem is in no way addressed by the Act. The following example of the potential pitfalls for a putative claimant must suffice but the reader will no doubt be able to think of others:

(a) The contractual term of the old lease expires and no steps are taken to bring the 1954 Act into play by service of any of the appropriate notices.

(b)   The errant tenant disappears, leaving unpaid a backlog of 'fixed charges' which the claimant is validly called upon to pay by way of the default notice procedure. He does so and asks for his overriding lease so that he can get back possession.

(c)   He is not able, however, to use the powers of the new lease to do either. The old lease is still in existence by virtue of statutory holding over which allows the overriding lease to be completed but it would seem that the new term could well, at best, equal the period of holding over (ie the old lease's 'term') plus three days. The latter is far too short a period for him to be able legally to re-enter to terminate the old lease and start trading. Neither can he, as tenant, serve a notice under the 1954 Act to terminate the overriding lease as he can only do this with effect from its contractual expiry date.

(d)   The landlord does nothing but require the claimant to comply with his covenants. If the latter was prudent, he would have obtained an indemnity from the errant tenant before assigning the old lease which he can now enforce to put the latter into liquidation but he still needs the liquidator to disclaim and the court to grant him a vesting order to get possession. If he was badly advised, of course, he will not have an indemnity and, as will be seen, with new tenancies, such a provision will not work in any case. In these circumstances, he will have to look elsewhere for a remedy.

Rule 16: the parties to business tenancies need to add to their list of matters to consider, whether taking up an overriding lease will, in practice, assist the prospective claimant in obtaining the additional flexibility meant to be provided thereby, so as to justify the expense.

In this context, your attention is drawn to the sections in Part III of this guide, starting on page 66, dealing with underleases and renewal of business tenancies.

(2)   With certain exceptions, the Act provides that all the covenants of the overriding lease (ie of the landlord as well as the tenant) are to be the same as those contained in the old lease (s 19(2)(b)).

The exceptions are:

Exception 1: the lease term will be as stated above (s 19(2)(a)) and the lease must also state that it has been granted under the Act as well as whether it is an old lease or a new tenancy (s 20(2) and see The Land Registration (Overriding Leases) Rules 1995, Appendix II p 151).

Exception 2: the landlord and tenant are allowed to agree any modifications they wish (s 19(2)(b)). This is clearly an important exception as, for instance, with turnover leases, there can obviously be covenants in the old lease the creation of which originally involved taking into account the individual characteristics of the parties but which were not expressed to be personal; if they were, please see below.

As general examples, the landlord in either a commercial or residential situation could have given covenants intended to run with the lease which in some way restrict its ability to deal with adjoining properties vested in it but which it was worthwhile giving, in order to entice the original tenant to take the old lease. Conversely, the claimant, when tenant, may have agreed to a very restricted user clause in order to get hold of premises that particularly suited his requirements but which no longer would be justified, by changed conditions in, say, his business or mode of living, if he were to go back into possession.

Equally, there are situations where a change in the law may have altered the thrust of a covenant from how it may have originally been seen to operate. Thus, recent consolidated judgments of the Court of Appeal, deciding arguments over the same point of interpretation of rent review clauses but dealt with differently in separate leases, will have radically altered the way such provisions will now be seen as compared with only the recent past.

Specifically, the position with old turnover leases, so prevalent in modern retail leases, must give concern to any landlord, unless whoever originally drafted them was sufficiently prescient, as we shall shortly see, to make them personal; even then, however, the problem is not necesarily solved. The grant of the overriding lease on the basis provided for in the Act could well leave the landlord, for example, no longer with the right of checking its previous tenant's trading records, as usually allowed for in turnover leases; it would have to depend on the claimant to do this.

This is not necessarily the end of it so far as retail leases are concerned. It has been normal policy with shopping centre leases to require tenants to keep open for trade during stated periods. Unless the claimant is lucky with the relevant wording he inherits from the old lease, he could, always provided the House of Lords eventually agree with the Court of Appeal's recent decision in *Cooperative Insurance Society Ltd v Argyll (Stores) Holdings Ltd* [1996] 09 EG 128, find himself the subject of a claim, not only for damages, but also now even for specific performance, in circumstances over which he has no direct control; exactly the sort of situation this whole procedure is intended to avoid.

> **Rule 17: an astute landlord, concerned about the terms of a possible overriding lease, will want to enter into negotiations with the relevant parties before the time for serving default notice expires since it is then that it should have the maximum leverage and room for manoeuvre. However, it *must* remember it only has six months from when the charge becomes due.**
>
> **In contrast, a former tenant might well be better off waiting to see whether he gets a default notice first and, if he does, then attempting to agree a package deal with his landlord-to-be.**

Exception 3: it seems that, if a covenant is, *in whatever terms*, expressed to be a personal one under the terms of the old lease (s 19(3)) or is spent and can no longer bite (s 19(4)(b)), there is no obligation on whichever of the landlord and the claimant wants to see it removed from the overriding lease to give way; the Act does not require its inclusion.

One question that needs answering is: what makes a covenant personal for this purpose? There seems to be plenty of scope for argument. For example, can it not be argued that any 'keep open' clause must, *per se*, be personal to some extent? If so, that would seem enough to bring it and other covenants with a similar connotation, eg regulating the landlord's conduct when controlling adjoining property, within the exception. Whilst, on the face of it, a covenant which is spent might appear easier to clearly identify, the answer might not necessarily be open and shut, particularly with building obligations, for instance, and possible latent defects.

Exception 4: often a lease contains matters which fall to be determined or otherwise operate by reference to its commencement. When transferring covenants containing such matters over from an old lease to the new overriding lease, they are to be amended, if they are not spent by then (s 19(4)(b)), so that the relevant part operates by reference to the start date of the new lease (s 19(4)(a)).

As with Exception 3, the Act neglects to clarify matters if there is a difference of opinion over interpretation here between the parties One can readily foresee genuine differences of opinion in interpreting the revision of clauses dealing with, say, breaks in the lease, rent review provisions or repairing or redecoration obligations, all of which may be claimed to operate in some way by reference to the old lease's term commencement.

However, it is well worth bearing in mind that the courts might well be loath to change the terms other than, say, where specifically required to in relation to the term commencement date, to avoid rewriting the bargain between the parties; they could well view the underlying purpose of an overriding lease, which it should adhere to as far as possible, to be merely the required substitution of the parties to give the claimant the intended extra scope of action to protect his position.

More difficulty, though, might be experienced with our turnover lease problem highlighted when dealing with Exception 2. If use of Exception 3 allows the landlord to go as far as saying it is not required at all to include turnover clauses in the new overriding lease because they were personal to the old lease, what replaces them as a basis of calculating rent? Whilst the logical answer might seem to be a rent calculated on the basis of the passing rent under the old now sub-lease, there is still to be resolved the provisions the landlord may say it requires to assure the turnover rent is being properly assessed and collected.

Rule 18: both in the context of Exceptions 3 and 4, until the courts resolve any uncertainty, a determined landlord, faced

with granting an overriding lease where it would rather not, might be tempted to take advantage of the situation (where it can) although it should remember its duty to complete the lease within a reasonable time. The claimant should not overlook these possible difficulties when deciding whether to exercise its right to the overriding lease.

Rule 19: if there is a need to deal with a repairing obligation by reference to the situation appertaining at the beginning of the new lease, the parties may well wish to consider agreeing a Schedule of Dilapidations at that time.

NB: One final thought to be especially borne in mind by a claimant when deciding whether to take up an overriding lease. As Customs and Excise presently see it, he gets no right of refund or set-off with regard to the VAT element of any debt he is required to discharge as a result of a default notice; it seems that they simply refuse to recognise it as a VAT payment. Once the claimant has his overriding lease, however, he can treat rent and other payments he makes in the normal way for VAT purposes.

Effect on tenant and his surety of subsequent lease variation

A brief outline of the liability of former tenants and guarantors, as it was thought to be prior to the passing of the Act, was given on pages 5 and 6 of this guide. Whilst the corresponding position of sureties could be in some doubt, a doubt perhaps strengthened by recent court decisions, it was generally thought that, at least, that of former tenants was simply unfair in that they were stuck with responsibility for most changes to the tenant's obligations after they had assigned, without their agreement having been obtained or, indeed, sought. Thus, the landlord could agree major changes to the lease requested of it by the current tenant, say, to the user provisions, in return for an increase in rent and/or a change in rent review terms, and it would have the comfort of knowing it could revert back to its earlier tenants in respect of those changed obligations.

This is no longer the case. The Act was negotiated to reduce the chances of both tenants and their sureties being caught out in this way, but only in respect of variations made *after* the Act's start up date (namely 1 January 1996) (ss 18(2) and (3)). However, within one week of the Act coming onto the statute book, the Court of Appeal not only changed the common law as it had been generally perceived for some years but also will have achieved the same objective as the Act, but only more so in so far as former tenants are concerned. As a change in the law, contrary to the Act, it operates on *any* variation, whenever made, but only as it affects tenants and *not* sureties.

In *Friends Provident Life Office v British Railways Board* [1995] 48 EG 106, the Court of Appeal looked at a situation where the defendants, the original tenants, were being sued for arrears incurred by an assignee but argued that the lease had been so substantially varied as to release them from liability. The assignees had wanted to sublet the property in parts to short-term occupiers whilst the lease would only have allowed occupation by a single tenant. In return for varying both the level of and the basis for calculating the rent, the landlord agreed to changes to the user and alienation provisions in the lease to enable the assignees to trade as they wanted.

Firstly, the court decided that the changes were not sufficiently clear and unequivocal to amount to a deemed surrender and re-grant of the lease, which would have automatically released the original tenants (and indeed any sureties) from liability, by reaffirming that it could only perceive increasing the length of the lease or the size of the property demised having this effect. But they also decided that this principle did not affect their conclusion that the original contractual obligations of the previous tenants were not altered by unforeseen variations to the lease to which they were not a party. In this case, therefore, the defendants were only held responsible for rent calculated at the initial level although the court's decision might well have been different if it had construed the variation as releasing the tenants from an obligation to pay the original lower rent altogether rather than, as it found, as the mere substitution of an obligation to pay an increased amount.

The most interesting consequence of the decision may be how it relates to rent reviews; an uplift following a review in line with the original lease terms must fall within the contemplation of the original tenant, but what happens if the rent review provisions are varied outside the arrangement originally provided for, and a much higher rent results? Assuming that he cannot successfully construe the variation as a release of the original terms, the original tenant might not be affected by the review at all or the court could equally revert back to the bargain he contracted for and impose on him a review based on those original terms.

So far as former tenants are concerned, the terms of the Act do not appear to extend as far as the Court of Appeal's judgment and, of course, do not operate retrospectively. However, it does give statutory authority to ensure that no former tenant (s 18(2)), *or his guarantor* (s 18(3)), can have his liability increased by changes which, when the tenant parted with his interest, the landlord was not obliged to agree to.

Such variations, whether effected by deed or otherwise, provided made after 1 January 1996 will not bind the earlier tenant or his surety. For them not to be affected, the variation must either be one the landlord at that time had 'an *absolute right to refuse*' consent to (s 18(4)(a)) or that it had such a right, however (since the time of the assignment by the former tenant claiming or through whom is claimed the benefit of this provision) taken away (s 18(4)(b)). This latter alternative is obviously intended to prevent a landlord doing a deal with its then tenant to remove the landlord's right of refusal where it exists (see next paragraph) and, thus, keep the former tenant, or, more likely now, his surety on the hook for later variations it and the tenant agree to.

In assessing whether the landlord has an absolute right to withhold consent to a change, the Act requires *all circumstances*, not just the wording of the lease and any collateral agreement, to be taken into account, including any relevant legislation (s 18(5)). This works against the former tenant. Thus, where the provisions of the

Landlord and Tenant Act 1927 operate on the clauses of the old lease on the relevant occasions and at the relevant times, eg by imputing reasonableness to the landlord's right to withhold consent to a proposed assignment or subletting or by preventing the landlord from stopping improvement works proposed by the tenant, wording in those clauses purporting to give the landlord an absolute right to object will not, under the Act, be sufficient to stop earlier tenants and sureties from being duly responsible for any variations to those clauses made without their consent.

This much may be clear. However, if a landlord has a right, whether express or implied, to refuse consent to a change of use when on reasonable grounds, is it so obvious this is not 'an absolute right to refuse' for the purposes of the Act where, say, the landlord agrees to vary the lease by allowing a use which it would clearly have been within its rights to refuse consent to? Once again, complications ensue when it comes to interpreting the Act in the light of what might happen in the real world, however obvious at first glance its purport might seem.

At least, on the face of it, when it comes to considering the position of a surety, matters will be much simpler. No such luck. Whilst the common law rule that a prejudicial variation to a guarantor's contractual obligations will release him still applies, provided he did not consent to the change or the guarantee document itself does not indicate to the contrary, recent court decisions have highlighted the difficulties of applying this rule in practice.

Parties to a guarantee should be extra vigilant when reviewing liability in the light of variations agreed or to be agreed, particularly as the Act itself contains its own catch if the guarantor wants to rely on it to, at least, restrict its liability; it only can do so in relation to a *former* tenant's obligations, not with regard to any guarantee obligations given on behalf of the tenant who actually agrees the change (s 18(3)).

One of those problems the Act does not address (but the Court of Appeal did) is the extent of the former tenant's (and a surety's) liability, assuming it is not bound by the variation. It seems that common law is left to its own devices and, for those former tenants who may have to struggle to interpret the affect on their position of the *Friends Provident* decision, reference should again be made to the earlier comments on the possible consequences of a subsequent change to the rent review arrangements.

> **Rule 20: from now on no variation proposed to a lease by a current tenant should be agreed to by a landlord until it has fully reviewed the effect it will have on the residual liability of any tenants and sureties further up the chain. Conversely, no such tenant or surety should pay on demand from a landlord, whether it be in receipt of a default notice or not, until it is satisfied, *inter alia*, that no relevant covenant has been varied in any manner subsequent to the appropriate disposal and that any such variation has not affected his liability.**

Rule 21: a prudent landlord should not risk having challenged the basis of its calculation of apportioned liability against such a tenant or surety, whether in a default notice or not. It is safer to serve a default notice for the full amount owed by the current tenant on the basis that this is the sum it 'intends' to recover. The Act does not impose any specific obligation on the landlord to actually seek recovery at that or any other level.

Postscript on old leases

This guide already contains a number of examples of ambiguities, both patent and latent, which arise from endeavouring to interpret the Act in the context of situations that are found in the real world and which, thus, appear ripe for future litigation. This is before we consider its further effect on *rent review clauses in old leases*, an area of landlord and tenant law replete with cases that have taxed the minds and, quite often, the patience of High Court judges in recent years.

This is because it has become standard practice, in the case mainly of rent reviews of commercial property, to provide that the market rent should be assessed on review through the mechanism of a series of assumptions, based on the premise that, on the rent review date, a new and, therefore, hypothetical lease is to be granted, mainly on the same terms and conditions as the actual lease, to a hypothetical new tenant. The courts in particular have recoiled against the introduction into such provisions of any more unreality than is strictly necessary, relying on what appears to be the growing doctrine of 'commercial reality'.

In the light of the above, it should not be surprising to find that much comment has already been engendered by the absence in the Act of any guidance as to how to assess its effect on a new, albeit hypothetical, tenancy, because deemed for the purpose of the rent review to have been granted after the Act's start up date, when it is stated to be in the same form, unless expressly provided otherwise, as the actual old lease.

The extent of the increased effect of the Act on a new tenancy, as compared with an old lease, specifically when considering the terms of a new tenancy's alienation clauses, should shortly become clear from this guide. It will be a brave man who is prepared to venture that it will have other than a sufficiently material effect on valuation issues where old leases were drawn up oblivious of the Act as to eventually tempt parties to litigate the issue in the High Court, even if, to the author, the odds seem, at this time, stacked on one answer being likely if the courts maintain their present line of thinking.

Part II: New tenancies

We now turn to all tenancies and leases within the Act granted after the Act's start up date, 1 January 1996, *except*, the reader will remember, those granted pursuant to an agreement, option, pre-emption right and court order in existence before that date or when an overriding lease follows on an old lease. This means, for example, that an order from the court for a new business lease made before the cut-off date gives rise to an old lease, even if not completed until afterwards, whilst one granted pursuant to an order after that date, as a new tenancy, must expressly take into account the changes we are now going to deal with.

For a start, these new tenancies, as we decided to call them, are affected by *all* of the Act's provisions, including those dealt with in detail above.

What this means, above all, is that *the privity of contract rule is abolished* for all new tenancies, thus fulfilling the original aim of the progenitors of the legislation. In addition, tenants, as mentioned, also get the benefit of the three innovations to the law introduced by the Act as it affects old leases: the right to an overriding lease and the inhibitions placed on landlords through the need for default notices plus the intended scope for reducing former tenant and surety liability as a result of lease variations.

Bearing in mind that the Act is a compromise, what do landlords get out of it, apart, of course, from the retention, albeit in a somewhat emasculated form, of the privity of contract rule for old leases?

Firstly, the consequences of the disappearance of privity of contract for tenants of new leases are themselves partly dissipated by the Act, particularly by the introduction of another new concept, that of *an authorised guarantee agreement*, of which more shortly.

Next, the abolition of the rule on privity of contract works both ways. Rarely in a modern lease does a landlord get away with just a covenant for quiet enjoyment. Whatever covenants it gives its tenant, whether it includes an obligation to keep part of the structure in repair or to provide other services, a landlord can now ask to be released from once it has assigned its reversion. This does not place it in as good a position as a tenant, whom the Act expressly provides is to be released automatically when he assigns, but the more onerous the landlord's obligations the more it needs to keep in the forefront of its mind the opportune moment to exercise this right.

However, leaving aside privity of contract for a moment, there is not much doubt that the main benefit the Act is intended to give landlords of commercial (not 'residential' or agricultural) property is the variation to the main statutory provision governing the control by such landlords of the tenant's ability to assign his lease. When the abolition by legislation of privity of contract was first seriously mooted, landlords were particularly exercised by the thought that the overriding requirement imposed on them by the Landlord and Tenant Act 1927 not to act unreasonably when exercising their discretion as to whether or not to give consent to a proposed assignment would unfairly fetter them even more than it already did, bereft as they would then be of the comfort of a guaranteed fall-back position against at least the original tenant.

In essence only, since the change will be dealt with in greater depth later, the Act amends s 19(1) of the 1927 Act to allow the parties to agree *in advance* the basis upon which the tenant can assign his lease without the landlord having to worry about whether it is in breach of the old test of reasonableness. However, as we shall see, landlords should beware; this can be very much of a double-edged sword. A great deal of time is being (and will be) devoted to how this issue can best be tackled in the light of the new latitude now given to landlords. The way the debate goes could well end up having a pivotal influence on the way tenancy (and lease) terms are structured in the future and, thus, on the investment market, reliant as it is on that structure for the income on which its health depends.

Before returning to this vitally important subject, we must look in more substantive detail at the consequences of the abolition of the privity of contract rule itself.

The end of privity

Introduction

It has to be borne in mind that a significant proportion of the Act, and thus of the time expended by its draftsmen, is taken up with the technical changes required not only to rescind the old rule and the legislation introduced years ago in response to it but also to replace it with an entirely new structure of law intended to encompass the basic principle that each tenant and, subject to the limits imposed by that structure, landlord under a new tenancy should be liable only whilst they actually hold their respective interests. They should not be responsible for the sins of their successors or, for that matter, their predecessors although, as we shall see, there are clear (and perhaps not so clear) exceptions to this.

It is not intended in this guide to deal with all the Act's technical provisions but rather to concentrate on the perceived practical consequences of their introduction. This does not mean that they can be ignored. For property law practitioners to do so could be fatal and others must be aware that pitfalls lie in wait for the unwary, reliant as he or she may be on formats that have long stood the test of time.

For example, in the section of the Act (s 3) which provides the technical building blocks for all that follows, and which can thus be easily ignored, the draftsmen have slipped in this subclause:

> Any landlord or tenant covenant of a tenancy which is restrictive of the user of land shall, as well as being capable of enforcement against an assignee, be capable of being enforced against any person who is the owner or occupier of any demised premises to which the covenant relates, even though there is no express provision in the tenancy to that effect (s 3(5)).

One can easily think of the possible implications of the above if not properly addressed at the time of drafting a new tenancy. In the case of a unit in a large residential scheme, for example, the landlord may have given its tenant purchaser of a long lease all the comfort it thought expedient to provide by way of a landlord covenant restricting possible use of other parts of the estate only to find, at some later date, a possible purchaser of its reversion objecting, because of the above, being saddled with a restriction it perceives as materially limiting its future ability to deal with those other parts of the estate. Equally, a tenant, say, of a unit in a shopping centre, will find himself directly responsible to another tenant who had long had a lease containing a landlord's covenant forbidding the user the tenant is proposing to employ for his new unit; he can only look to hope to recover his loss from an errant landlord.

However, it is equally feasible to argue that these inferences are taking things too far; stress can be put on the word 'capable' to show that the subclause is only meant to make it possible for the covenant to affect another 'owner or occupier', even where there is no express provision to that effect, but is not meant to override the normal rules that would otherwise apply.

There are other potential pitfalls and ambiguities one could amplify from the technical side and some are of sufficient practical importance to warrant mention below in considering the consequences of the legislation.

> **Rule 22: notwithstanding what follows, unless you feel absolutely confident that you are right, any prudent party to a landlord and tenant situation anxious to avoid an unwanted liability should not hesitate to seek further advice as to the possible consequences of what he or she wants to agree before committing himself, herself or any principal.**

Tenant's release

(1) Where a tenant assigns the whole of his interest in a tenancy, the Act provides for his automatic release from his covenants (remember the wider definition of these and especially that they can come from collateral agreements as well as the tenancy document itself) from the date of assignment plus the simultaneous

end of the benefit to him of the landlord covenants (s 5(2)). The same thing happens to his guarantor to the extent necessary (s 24(2)).

(2) In the perhaps unlikely event of a tenant assigning part of his interest (most leases up to now have prevented part assignments by the tenant), the Act allows him (and his surety) to be released in relation to that part only, ie he would be released from the usual obligations for repair and user so far as they can be attributed to the part assigned but also lose the benefit of such landlord covenants as can be attributed in the same way (s 5(3)).

However, the Act provides for a different procedure for a covenant, relating very likely to money, which cannot be split between the areas assigned and retained; what it calls a 'non-attributable covenant'. Here, both *assignor* and *assignee* are bound by it, the liability being apportioned between themselves as they may agree (including full indemnity) (s 9). Both parties, within four weeks of the assignment, can serve a notice on the landlord and/or some other party entitled to enforce the covenant in question, applying for the apportionment to be binding on the recipient (s 10(1) and see Form 7 of Appendix II, p 132). The latter has four weeks to serve its notice objecting (Part II, Form 7, Appendix II, p 135). Otherwise it is bound by the apportionment (s 10(2)). If it does object and continues to do so, a county court decides whether it is reasonable for the recipient to be bound (s 10(2)).

(3) It is important to bear in mind that the tenant does not get released if the assignment in question has taken place in breach of covenant or by operation of law (for example, death, vesting of new trustees, including a trustee in bankruptcy, or vesting following a company dissolution or compulsory purchase) (s 11(2)(a)). The assignment is valid but the tenant has to wait until the next assignment not caught by this rule to be released. In the meantime, he, as the former tenant, and any surety he may have provided, are subject to the default notice procedure with the attendant right to an overriding lease.

At least one practical difficulty emanates from this rule. What happens in an asset sale situation where, for example, confidentiality is of special concern because of Stock Exchange requirements? It is not viable to get multifarious consents before an agreement is consummated in such circumstances but the vendor will still want to be released from his obligations. If a lease allows subletting without consent, that might be an answer but, otherwise, a vendor will have to insist on a conditional contract, requiring him to get landlord's consent before completion, which, in turn, is likely to complicate the drafting of the sale agreement.

(4) When an assignee takes over the new tenancy, he does not as a result take over any liability or rights under covenants 'in relation to any time before the assignment' (s 23(1)) unless any such rights (not liabilities) are expressly assigned to him (s 23(2)); even if they are duly assigned, it may not do him a great deal of good as elsewhere the Act also states that 'a party who ceases to be entitled to the benefit of a covenant by virtue of the Act [ie the assignor to the landlord covenants] does not thereby have affected his rights arising from a breach of

the covenant occurring before he ceases to be so entitled'. Is this yet another example of the Act leaving an apparent ambiguity to be resolved by the courts, this time as to who the rights are vested in, bearing in mind the anti-avoidance provision tells us that virtually all 'agreements' (as it defines them) will be void if they purport to 'exclude, *modify* or otherwise frustrate the operation of any provision of this Act' (s 25(1)(a))?

Note that the assignor's release from a covenant by virtue of the Act is expressly stated not to affect any liability he has arising from a breach of such covenant occurring beforehand (s 24(1)), eg arrears of rent accrued due before the assignment.

> **Rule 23: a prudent landlord will want to consider the condition of the demised property very carefully on a proposal for an assignment being put to it so that it can fix the tenant (and any surety) with any liability by the time any assignment takes place. In his turn, the tenant should review the potential for liability carefully before he starts committing himself to assignment procedures; he may regret it otherwise.**

(5)   Of course, whilst they remain landlord and tenant, the respective parties are bound by the landlord and tenant covenants relating to the demise assigned to them (s 3(2)(ii) and (3)(ii)) but provided that, *inter alia*, immediately before the assignment to that party the covenant bound the assignor (s 3(2)(i) and (3)(i)).

Yet one more potentially very dangerous, because unintended, pitfall arises from this proviso. Maybe, say, the landlord had agreed to waive a tenant covenant whilst the assignor of the tenancy had remained in possession but not further or otherwise. It seems clear that it would not, unless vigilant over the terms of any waiver, be able to enforce the covenant against the assignee or his successors either.

> **Rule 24: even more care than before now needs to be taken before agreeing or allowing any waiver to avoid unintended consequences. In this context, refer also to para (8) below.**

(6)   Where there is a *third party* (not a guarantor) to a new tenancy which covenants to discharge a particular function for the tenant's benefit or has the benefit of covenants which entitle it to enforce a particular right against the tenant, for the Act's purposes they are respectively treated as landlord covenants and tenant covenants. Thus, the tenant on assignment can be expected to be released from enforcing or being liable for them and, in respect of the former, can pass on the right to sue to the assignee (s 12).

The most likely third party to be found in such circumstances is a management company and the above is, therefore, especially pertinent in both residential and commercial situations involving multi-tenancies.

Rule 25: if the management company is or can become at arm's length from the landlord, for its protection it needs contractual rights to receive at least prior notification of all prospective dealings with the tenant's interest so that, like the landlord, it can assess its position with regard to the anticipated release and transfer of tenant covenants.

(7) Remember that there are provisions in the Act governing the position if, for example, you find the covenantors are joint tenants (s 13) or where a tenant's covenant or a right of re-entry can be enforced by a third party other than the reversioner who, 'as the holder of the immediate reversion, is entitled for the time being to the rents and profits under the tenancy' (s 15(1)(a)) (receiver, trustee in bankruptcy or liquidator but not the tenant's mortgagee in possession who is expressly given rights to pursue and be liable to the requisite parties for any default as if it had been that tenant (s 15(3))).

(8) More important to bear in mind, however, is what happens to covenants expressed (*in whatever terms*) to be personal to any person (s 3(6)(a)) or which are registrable but not registered (s 3(6)(b)).

Nothing, says the Act, can make them enforceable after being transmitted by or against any other party, ie the burden of a covenant personal to the original tenant or not registered under the 1925 legislation when it should have been would appear to die with his assignment provided the latter is not in breach or it is made by operation of law, when it should die next time round. For comment on the wide nature of the definition of a personal covenant in the Act please refer to Exception 3 from page 19 of this guide.

Rule 26: parties to the original negotiation especially should bear in mind that this might again make a covenant die when it might not be the intention unless the covenantee watches things very closely.

However, remember that any waiver (or, indeed, release) of a non-personal covenant which was itself expressed in whatever terms to be personal to the assignor will not be effective in preventing the covenant in its original form from being passed over to an assignee (s 3(2)). This assumes that the waiver comes within the Act's very wide definition of a covenant (see s 28(1) and s 3(6)(a)). What also needs to be borne in mind in this context is Rule 24 and the remarks leading up to it.

Bearing in mind the wide range of documents that can include tenant covenants, it needs to be carefully noted that they include specifically collateral agreements (s 28(1)) so that obligations given under a rent deposit or bond agreement by or through the tenant are equally affected by the new rules.

(9) The technical changes introduced by the Act plus its anti-avoidance provisions, of which more later, are clearly meant to ensure that implied indemnity covenants from new tenants, still relevant as they may be where old leases are concerned, become redundant in favour of the landlord as part of the process of abolition of privity of contract for new tenancies.

Whilst implied indemnity covenants are expressly abolished so far as the assignor is concerned also (s 14), there is nothing in the Act to stop the former tenant asking for an express indemnity from his assignee in relation to breaches of covenant whilst the latter remains the tenant.

Why, however, should the former tenant want this?

Landlords have two ways of obtaining direct covenants from guarantors to the assignee, one of which provides the main exception to the rule that a tenant is not responsible for the actions of his successor in new tenancies and this answers the question as to why he should have made the provision of an indemnity as part of the contractual package with his assignee.

The two ways are:

(a) obtaining the right to require a proposed assignee to provide *a third-party guarantee* or guarantees of his obligations. As already indicated, and as we shall see in greater detail later, there is absolutely nothing to prevent a new tenancy's alienation provisions providing for this on whatever terms the parties agree and, even if the point is not covered specifically, it could, in any case, be viewed as a reasonable requirement of the landlord when an assignment of the lease is proposed for its approval.

There are no fetters as to the form of the guarantee in the Act but it can only operate to the extent that the tenant being guaranteed remains liable for his covenants (s 24(2)) contra a guarantor of a tenant under an old lease who can separately remain liable until the end of the term.

Do remember that the provisions in the Act relating to default notices and overriding leases will *not* apply to the guarantor under his guarantee whilst the assignee he is guaranteeing remains the tenant in possession.

Rule 27: the need for guarantors should clearly be an essential part of the consideration of alienation clauses which, as will be seen later, is an exercise that must be carried out by all with property interests.

Even more important should be a consideration by all landlords of the need to provide in such clauses for the giving by an assignor of:

(b) *Authorised Guarantee Agreements* (henceforth called 'AGA' or 'AGAs').

The option of requiring an AGA is the only exception to the new rule that an assignor is automatically released from his liabilities after completing an assignment not carried out in breach or by operation of law.

The original prime objection from the British Property Federation (BPF) to the introduction of this new principle to the land law applicable to England and Wales was the sudden removal of this long-accepted comfort to a landlord the very first time his current tenant was able to assign. The compromise soon mooted was to allow it to keep the assignor on the hook until the next but one assignment. In essence the AGA is the vehicle introduced by the Act to enable the landlord to have the benefit of this compromise by giving it the opportunity, especially when agreeing the terms of new tenancies, of requiring the current tenant for the time being, as a condition of any subsequent assignment being permitted, to guarantee his assignee's obligations *but only* whilst the latter remains in his turn bound to comply with the tenant covenants.

What are the circumstances that must be adhered to if the landlord is to be able to require the tenant to enter into an AGA?

- The tenancy must contain a covenant prohibiting assignment (whether absolute or conditional) without the *consent* of the landlord or some other person (eg superior landlord) (s 16(3)(a));

- Such consent is given subject to a '*lawfully imposed*' condition that the tenant is to enter into an AGA (s 16(3)(b)); and

- The AGA is entered into by the tenant in pursuance of that condition (s 16(3)(c)). (The AGA should, therefore, contain a statement to that effect.)

If the tenant has had his obligations to the landlord in the new tenancy guaranteed by a third party, does the above (or anything else in the Act) prevent that third party from being required also to guarantee the tenant's obligations under a resultant AGA?

Yet another question to which the Act gives no clear answer by seeming to ignore the possibility.

As already pointed out, a third-party guarantee can only bite to the extent that the tenant being covered remains liable under the Act. Without specifically referring to a surety in this context, the Act does seem to provide for his complete release on a valid assignment of the whole of the interest of the tenant he is guaranteeing (s 24(2)) whilst there is nothing in the Act that allows for his obligations to be extended to cover that tenant's obligations if the latter is then required to enter into an AGA.

It has to be asked whether it is, therefore, a breach of the Act's anti-avoidance provisions to resurrect that guarantee in another guise. For a start, the Act does state that the rules of law relating to guarantees (in particular those relating to the release of sureties) are, *subject to its terms*, to be treated no differently in relation to an AGA to any other guarantee agreement (s 16(8)). With this in mind, it can be argued, on a strict interpretation of the Act's wording (see s 24(2)(b)), that the guarantor's release from his obligations on the tenant assigning does not extend to an obligation to underwrite the tenant's covenants when he enters into the AGA; he is stated as being only released from an obligation 'imposing any liability or penalty in the event of a *failure to comply*' with the relevant tenant covenant. The original guarantee given by the third party could, on this basis, if very carefully drawn up, protect the landlord by specifically encompassing the tenant complying with his covenant and taking up an AGA.

However, this difficult issue has already, in the Act's short life, given rise to a great deal of controversy and the above interpretation of how the Act should work is known to be far from universally accepted. Therefore, the danger of a claim being made that a requirement that a tenant's surety continue to act as such when that tenant enters into an AGA is, at least, *ultra vires* must be recognised. The third party should, on the other hand, bear in mind that, if he refuses to join in on the ground that such an obligation does not bind him, the landlord may, in consequence, validly refuse consent to the proposed assignment, thus leaving the third party open to an action for damages from an aggrieved tenant.

This whole question seems to be as certain as any other arising from the Act to lead to litigation.

> **Rule 28: to avoid the possibility of a later argument, at least until such time as the issue is satisfactorily resolved in the courts, the landlord will need to take even greater care than it would otherwise have done to see that it gets the best available covenant on the line as the tenant.**

What does 'lawfully imposed' mean?

The Act does not define the term but some assumptions can be made unless and until a court directs otherwise.

Clearly, if a tenancy includes an absolute prohibition against an assignment, the landlord can impose such conditions as it wishes, including the need for an AGA, before giving consent.

There appears to be no obvious reason why an express obligation on the tenant to provide an AGA before an assignment can proceed will not work. Under the new rules on alienation introduced by the Act, this can be expressed either as a condition to be fulfilled before consent can be given or as something the absence of which allows the landlord to withhold its consent or, indeed, to give further consideration to its decision (s 22('1A')).

If, however, the terms, including this one, relating to consent to an assignment are not specified, the landlord, as we shall see, is still required to act reasonably and it will be a matter for individual speculation and consideration at the time whether the particular circumstances entitle the landlord to 'lawfully impose' a condition requiring an AGA before the tenant's deal can proceed.

Even more litigation could be in prospect. The circumstances of the time might seem to dictate what might be considered 'lawful' for the landlord to impose as a condition but the absence of any mention of the AGA itself might well be used by the tenant as at least putting the onus on the landlord to justify its subsequent introduction as a condition.

Rule 29: it is likely that landlords will attempt to make a specific requirement for an AGA as a condition to an assignment a standard feature, at least in rack rent new tenancies or where there is going to be a material service charge or other substantive obligations for fixed charges for the current tenant to meet. In fact, all landlords concerned to protect their position against the tenant for the time being should aim to include this as a specific condition in all new tenancy agreements unless it is going to preserve to itself an absolute right to say no.

What form does the AGA have to take?

Provided a few rules are followed, it can be any form so that, in principle, there seems no reason why the guarantor, whether he be the former tenant, or his surety if 'persuaded' lawfully to join the AGA, cannot extend the default notice procedure to cover any claim against him, not just a 'fixed charge'. However, as paragraph (d) below makes clear, the landlord cannot remove the need to comply with the procedure where a 'fixed charge' is concerned (s 17(1)).

Thus, an AGA can guarantee the performance of tenants' covenants by the tenant's assignee to any extent, eg, as noted, by cutting down the previous tenant's liability under the AGA by making it all subject to the six-months rule, *save* only for the following:

(a) It must not impose any liability, restriction or other requirement, of whatever nature, relating to any time *after* the assignee is itself released under the Act (s 16(4)(b)).

(b) It can only guarantee the *assignee's* obligations, nobody else's, eg his mortgagee or surety or an original underlessee (s 16(4)(a)).

    This might encourage, of course, an assignee to do a deal with his assignor to shorten his period as tenant by assigning straight on to, say, an associate. The landlord will have to look very carefully at the alienation provisions, as we shall see, to try and prevent this from happening, assisted, no doubt, by the greater scope given to it by the Act's provisions on alienation.

(c) It can, it seems, impose liability no more onerous on the guarantor than as a sole or principal debtor (s 16(5)). This, the usual level of liability imposed in a modern form of guarantee, was thought to be sufficient to ensure that a guarantor would not be automatically released by alterations or indulgences granted to the assignee. As was mentioned earlier in this guide the effectiveness of this method has recently been thrown into some doubt, and expert advice on this subject should be sought, particularly since, as has been seen, the Act expressly provides for the rules as to the release of sureties to apply to AGAs (s 16(8)), including, as a result, the Act's own provisions regarding variations to tenancies.

(d) As already mentioned, the landlord cannot remove from the guarantor in the AGA (or elsewhere) the right given to him by the Act to rely on the restrictions imposed by the default notice procedure when he is called on to pay a 'fixed charge' (see page 6 onwards) (s 17(1)). All the restrictions on recovery imposed by the default notice procedure *will* apply, do remember, as also will the consequent rights to an overriding lease if the AGA guarantor pays.

The reader will be able to glean from the relevant sections of this guide those aspects especially pertinent to the AGA guarantor's position but the following points may be of assistance:

(i) Mention has already been made on more than one occasion of the importance of the six-months time limit, time, indeed, being of the essence, in which the landlord's interests can be protected by the serving of a default notice and that the period is stated as running from 'the date when the charge shall become due' (s 17(2)).

Bearing in mind that the default notice procedure covers any guarantor of a former tenant who is found, because the latter's assignment failed to release him (see para (3) on page 27), to remain liable for the performance of a tenant covenant under which a fixed charge is payable, not just a former tenant in his guise as an AGA guarantor, the question has to be asked whether the six months, in such cases, is meant to run from when the debt becomes due from the original obligant or from the surety; the dates may not be the same.

The Act does not differentiate and, rather than rely on how the courts might interpret its intentions, it is strongly suggested that careful draftsmanship be employed to ensure that there is a consistent start date for liability to commence between the principal obligant and his respective surety.

(ii) The landlord should also remember, when drawing up its new tenancy, that the more it provides for the payment of monies under it to be reserved as 'rent' the more it brings them, as a result, within the definition of a 'fixed charge' (s 17(6)) and thus within the default notice procedure irrespective of whether they come within under one of the other relevant definitions.

> **Rule 30: the landlord may be too clever for its own good if it puts every potential recovery down as 'rent' without thinking it through, especially if it does not intend to allow an assignor tenant to widen his escape route beyond that provided by a 'fixed charge'.**

Is it possible for there to be more than one AGA at a time?

Yes. When the former tenant only gets released on a later assignment because the first one took place in breach or by operation of law, he, plus the assignor in the usual way, can then be required to give an AGA. However, he cannot be asked to give it alone, it must be done jointly with the assignor (s 16(6)).

Can a tenant be required to enter into an AGA more than once?

Yes. The Act expressly permits, including in the above circumstances, an AGA to contain a clause requiring the former tenant to take up a new tenancy of no greater length and no more onerous than the previous one in the event of the latter being disclaimed through an assignee's insolvency (s 16(5)(c)). The tenant can be then required to give another AGA when he assigns the second tenancy in the same way as he can if the first is revested in him instead through the vesting order procedure (s 16(7)(a)).

Here things do become somewhat technical. In this context, the recent decision of the House of Lords in *Hardcastle v Barbara Attenborough Associates Ltd* (see page 5) may well have muddied these particular waters. The way they have now set out how statute is to be reinterpreted, the AGA guarantor remains liable following such disclaimer in any event, presumably unless he obtains a sufficiently clearly expressed contractual right to walk away in such circumstances. Further, in probably the first reference in a major judgment to the Act, Lord Nicholls specifically mentioned the fact that a guarantor (under an old lease as well) 'may be entitled to an overriding lease' as a result of disclaimer, ie one assumes subject only to the default notice procedure being followed. This is especially appropriate where the surety does not, or cannot, even by applying out of time, get a vesting order.

That a surety should endeavour to do one or the other if he wants to obtain some return from the property is made very obvious by Lord Nicholls in his wide-ranging and admirably clear speech, considering that he was reinterpreting difficult legislation which has caused many problems over the years. He understands statute as indicating, 'not without artificiality', as he rightly says, that 'when the lease is disclaimed it is determined but the rights and liabilities of others, such as guarantors and original tenants, are to remain *as though* the lease had continued and not been determined'!

Thus, on the one hand, 'unless a vesting order is made, after disclaimer there will be no subsisting lease and the property will be empty and vacant'. On the other, it is not 'determined' so as to stop the guarantor getting his overriding lease in the appropriate circumstances (remember the quote from s 19(7) conveniently set out earlier on page 15) whilst there is, Lord Nicholls tells us, a continuing liability on him (and any others affected, he should remember) to perform the tenant covenants until and unless whomsoever is the landlord enters upon the property and takes back possession. Exactly what is the status in all this of the new lease that we have seen an AGA guarantor can be contractually required to take up must, at this stage, be unclear if it is (as the Act provides – s 16(5)(c)(i)) to be for a term not exceeding that of the disclaimed lease. However, as a statutory right the landlord might be entitled to feel a degree of confidence that it will be upheld if included in the AGA.

> **Rule 31: it should be clear from all the comments above that it would probably be in the parties' interest, nearly as much for the tenant's side as for the landlord's, if a condition in a new tenancy requiring an AGA on an assignment made reference to the form of the AGA to be as attached to the tenancy.**

The assignor is reminded of the need to obtain the right to an indemnity from the new tenant before he agrees to assign so that he has the opportunity to retrieve any claim he later has to meet under his AGA.

Landlord's release

As has already been pointed out, landlords can also get released from landlord covenants on an assignment of a new tenancy's reversion but this is not intended to happen automatically (s 7(2) and (3)). They must rely on their tenants' agreeing or, otherwise, go to court to persuade it that it is reasonable for the landlord to be released (s 8(2)). It is a valuable right and, although the procedure can be long-winded, should always be considered at the relevant time as an opportunity for the landlord to divest itself of contingent liabilities that could otherwise come back to haunt it, including any, say, outstanding construction liabilities under Agreements for Lease; it cannot be stressed too often that landlord covenants encompass these for the purposes of the Act (s 28(1)).

Rule 32: anybody thinking of becoming a landlord of a new tenancy should check particularly carefully for outstanding obligations given by any reversioner under an Agreement for Lease which will bind unless personal or not covered by registration when they should have been.

The right is important, even though the procedure can be cumbersome, as it provides a landlord which has divested itself of an asset by assignment of the reversion with the opportunity, then and at the time of all relevant future assignments, of divesting itself of the concomitant liabilities with a constant right of appeal, failing agreement with the other contractual party.

Once it is agreed that the landlord should be released, it is backdated to the time when the relevant assignment took place (s 8(3)).

On any such release of the landlord's obligations under its relevant covenants, there is, in most cases, a simultaneous cessation of its right to benefit from equivalent tenant covenants (s 6(2)(b)) but see below.

When can the landlord apply to be released?

It gets more than one bite at the cherry:

(1) When it wishes to assign its reversion (or part of it), it has *four weeks from the date of the relevant assignment* to serve a notice in the form prescribed by regulation (see Forms 3 and 4 of the Schedule to the Landlord and Tenant (Covenant) Act 1995 (Notices) Regulations 1995 Appendix II, pp 112 and 117 respectively) or in a form substantially to the same effect on the appropriate tenant (s 8(2)(a)).

The landlord *must* assume that the four weeks is non-extendible.

However, it seems, it can decide the extent to which it wishes to be released (s 8(1)) so that it could, for example, retain the standard obligation for quiet enjoyment but ask to be released from its liability to repair or provide a tenant with services.

The above needs to be borne in mind because yet another quirk in the Act's drafting appears to provide for the simultaneous end of the landlord's rights to benefit from the tenant covenants but only following a request which leads to it being released from *all* its covenants (s 6(2)(b)). However, the landlord may have to be somewhat subtle in its approach. Thus, if the tenant is awake and the landlord needs to apply to the court for a direction that its request is reasonable to be released, there would seem, in the case of the example quoted in the previous paragraph, every chance that the court might not agree with it.

With this in mind, the position becomes even more complicated when one takes into account that the Act does make one thing clear, namely that, on an assignment, whether it involve the reversion or the tenant's interest, the assignee, by virtue of the Act, cannot automatically take over any rights (or liability) arising from a covenant it inherits as a result in relation to the period prior to the assignment (s 23(1)). Even though the rights to enforce the same can, nonetheless, be expressly assigned (s 23(2)), there remains a problem if this exception is not properly dealt with in the contractual arrangements and there is, in any event, no provision for the assignee to take over the burden of liabilities in relation to the earlier period in the same way. Further, the Act states that a right of re-entry in a new tenancy, from which the right to forfeit also flows, can be exercisable by the landlord's assignee in relation to a breach occurring before the assignment provided that breach had not been waived or released by the time the assignment occurred (ss 4 and 23(3)).

Remember that, if different parts of the premises to be assigned are held by different tenants, eg you have a multi-tenanted building, *each* has to be served with a notice (s 8(4)(a)), plus a management company or other third party liable by covenant to discharge any function with respect to the demise (but not guarantor) if it has rights against the landlord (s 12(3)(4) and (5)).

Just as important, there could be yet one more hidden trap lying in wait for the unwary landlord. Bear in mind, where dealing with more than one tenancy, that landlords do not have this right under the Act to go to court for a release where a tenant holds under an old lease. If one or more such tenants do not agree to let the landlord off, it stays on the hook with regard to its obligations so far as they are concerned which might well influence the court's decision where it does have jurisdiction.

(2) If it failed to get released for whatever reason the first time round when it was the assignor, eg it forgot, decided it preferred to keep the benefit of the tenant covenants as mentioned above or failed to get the tenant's consent or the court's declaration that its release was reasonable, the by now former landlord, assuming it is still bound by landlord covenants, ie has not been wholly released voluntarily

by the tenant in the meantime, can apply, again within four weeks of a subsequent assignment (time of the essence, remember), to the extent necessary (or required) to be released (s 7(2) and (3) and see Forms 5 and 6, Appendix II, pp 122 and 127 respectively).

It can apply on *any* subsequent assignment irrespective of how many times it has failed in previous applications (s 7(6)(b)) but it must do so within the four weeks following the date of the relevant assignment (s 8(1)).

NB:

(a)   The landlord does not have to wait for the assignment to take place before serving its request notice; the Act specifically states it can be served beforehand (s 8(1)). All the Act requires the notice to inform the tenant of in this respect is that an assignment is proposed until it is effected when that fact alone suffices by way of information (s 8(1)(a) see Forms 3–6, Appendix II). The tenant's consent, whether given or implied (or, indeed the court' determination), before the assignment is completed will not make the release effective until that completion (s 8(3)).

(b)   There are provisions governing a part assignment of the reversion by the landlord or former landlord, an occurrence likely to be found more often than with a tenant (s 6(3) and 7(3) and see Forms 4 and 6, Appendix II above). The notice procedures and rules outlined in this part of the note are all relevant but only to the extent that landlord covenants fall to be complied with in relation to any premises comprised in the relevant assignment (ss 6(3)(b) and 7(3) and note s 7(5)).

As a result, one can envisage difficulties with, say, a substantial multi-purpose building with common areas, such as entrances, staircases and roofs, and services, for example refuse collection and fire alarm systems, which the landlord has retained control of and covenants to maintain; it would not matter if the landlord ran a management company which owned the relevant areas and provided the services as its covenants are deemed for this purpose to be 'landlord covenants' (s 12(2)(b)).

If the landlord wants to sell off its reversion in separate pieces, it can only get released from its liability (and release the assignee from its liability to help discharge its proportion of the resultant cost) so far as each individual disposal is concerned. Unless all sales of leases were satisfactorily synchronised, one can easily envisage problems in persuading tenants and, ultimately, the courts, that the landlord's release will not unfairly prejudice tenants' ability to ensure their rights in relation to the common parts and services can be protected: it is certainly likely to add complications to the method by which they can thereafter enforce such rights.

These complications are caused, of course, by the fact that, in so far as the landlord covenants do not fall to be complied with in relation to the assignment of the part in question, the landlord cannot ask to be released (s 9(6)) but it should be remembered that the provisions (ss 9 and 10) governing 'non-attributable covenants' referred to in para (2) on page 27 of this guide do apply to all such covenants outside the ambit of the landlord's own assignment – see Form 8, Appendix II, p 137. This procedure may, therfore, provide an answer to our problem but not necessarily to the complications. Certainly it needs very careful watching.

(c) The Act specifically provides that s 3(3A) of the Landlord and Tenant Act 1985 will continue to operate (s 26(2)). This means that, even when the procedures outlined here have all been successfully completed, the former landlord would remain liable until the tenant has been notified of the new landlord's name and address. It should ensure contractually (if not physically) that this is done.

> **Rule 33: from what has already been stated, let alone what is to follow, a shrewd landlord will appreciate the need to think carefully, rather than joyfully jump in, before serving its notice. But there may be little point if the landlord does not ensure it can put into effect if it so decides the mechanics of serving its notice when the time comes.**
>
> **To do this, it needs to know on what address to serve the notice and, of course, when an assignment is planned, when it takes place and to whom. Provided it gets fully relieved when it first assigns, there should be no problem but the original landlord must ensure, for the benefit of its successors as well if it wants to protect the value of its investment, that all former landlords under the new tenancy will have the means of obtaining this information in case they may want to serve a notice on the then current tenant. The latter needs to be under an obligation in the tenancy or lease to supply all such parties with their address for service for the time being, not just their actual landlord.**
>
> **All assignors should always obtain in the assignment documentation appropriate contractual assurances and indemnities to have ascertained and passed on this information up the line as necessary plus appropriate notice of any anticipated and completed assignment of the reversion in sufficient time for the appropriate action to be taken.**
>
> **In turn, a prudent successor in title to the reversion will want to know what its assignor and any predecessors might do and, in fact, does so that it can consider any possible implications.**

What happens after the notice has been served?

(1) The tenant has just *four weeks* starting when the notice on him is served to send the landlord (or former landlord) a counter-notice objecting to the release to

the extent proposed in the first notice (s 8(2)(a) and see Part II, Forms 3–6, Appendix II). If he does not, the tenant will be taken as having agreed to the release as proposed even by doing nothing, *so tenants, beware*; you don't have a lot of time to make up your mind.

(2) Unless the tenant withdraws in writing his objection to the landlord's notice before the hearing (s 8(2)(c)), a county court will decide whether the proposed release in that notice is reasonable (s 8(2)(b)). The tenant should bear in mind that, if he loses in court, he is almost certainly going to have to bear the landlord's legal costs.

> **Rule 34: while the tenant should always be safe rather than sorry and, thus, give the notice in time if in any doubt, he does not want to end up in court unnecessarily, particularly if he believes the former landlord is going to be able to produce some pretty convincing evidence of the new landlord's *bona fides*. However, in any event, he may well consider the cost implications worth it if he believes he has sufficient room for manoeuvre to negotiate a better deal.**

> **Tenants (but also present and former landlords) should note that there is nothing in the Act which expressly prevents them agreeing their own terms of release with landlords at any time.**

What is the position once the relevant landlord is released?

The position of the landlord is virtually identical with that of a released tenant and, thus, the reader is asked to refresh his memory by reverting back to the note starting on page 26 under the heading of 'Tenant's release' and ending after para (8) on page 29; you might want to ignore the last part of para (6). Otherwise, save where the wording used in para (5) clearly makes this unnecessary, references to 'the tenant' should in this case be to the landlord (or former landlord as the case may be) and vice versa with references to 'the landlord'. So far as para (9) is concerned, a third-party guarantee can technically be sought by a tenant. If able to obtain one, the notes starting on page 29 will apply but no landlord can be required to take up an AGA.

What is the position until the landlord is released?

Obviously it can be different from that of the tenant and, furthermore, different from that appertaining previously because of the wholesale rebuilding of the legal structure on this subject.

The effect of all the changes for new tenancies is to allow for one or more landlord covenants to bind the landlord, whether they are found in the body of a lease, tenancy agreement, agreement for such or a collateral agreement such as a concession agreement from the landlord (s 28(1)), not only whilst still having the reversion to the new tenancy vested in it but, unlike the vast majority of tenants with tenant covenants, even after it has parted with its interest, until and unless it gets a final release.

It is important to remember, though, that a covenant does not bind a successor landlord in any case where it is *a personal one not inherited or a covenant that should have been registered to bind it* (s 3(6)). Also, one more reminder that 'covenants' here encompass a term, condition and obligation. Thus, the terms of a collateral side letter containing, say, concessions from the landlord on rent, come within the ambit of the definition, even if not expressed to be covenants.

> **Rule 35: Landlords need to review how they deal with collateral side letters.**
>
> **In particular, they need to ensure they are expressed in clear terms to be personal to the particular tenant to avoid any later argument as to whether they bind a successor.**
>
> **On the other hand, a landlord may well need to make it equally clear that any 'landlord covenants' which act as a waiver of tenant's obligations in the lease are not personal to it only and cannot be regarded as not binding its successors of title, a point recently highlighted by the Court of Appeal, but also, if it wants the obligations to continue to bind the tenant's successors, that the waiver ceases before any assignment (see para (5) and Rule 24 on page 28.**
>
> **Such side letters also need to take full account of the limits imposed on the recovery of old debts through the default notice procedure.**
>
> **Rule 36: for their part, tenants (and would–be tenants) should remember to be extremely cautious over the wording of landlord's covenants which are of material value to their interest so as to avoid it being claimed against them that the covenant is personal and that the landlord is, thus, automatically released on an assignment of its reversion.**

We are left with yet another of the Act's anomalies. As we have seen, the benefit of tenant covenants can stay with a landlord until it gets rid of all its liability by due release (s 6(2)(b)). Thus, unless the right to sue is sorted out between the parties, there can be more than one party entitled to enforce the tenant's obligations, the present landlord plus any predecessors yet to be fully released, whilst the Act gives no obvious indication that the former should have priority.

That may well be how the courts would interpret it but it is not difficult to envisage scenarios where a former landlord might have a genuine grouse. If the current landlord is not, say, providing the services it is meant to give the tenant, who is duly pursuing his previous landlord perfectly legitimately instead, surely the latter will argue that it should be entitled to a prior claim for recovery of at least the service charge. Who is to say that it will not ask for the rent itself if it feels its position *vis-à-vis* the current landlord sufficiently inequitable?

> **Rule 37: the above indicates the care that a tenant may need to take before acting on a request to agree a landlord's release whilst not forgetting the need to respond within four weeks.**
>
> **Even more, it accentuates the care that may have to be taken before discharging the tenant's monetary or other fixed charge obligations. The party doing so could argue that they want in return from the proposed recipient an indemnity (from a satisfactory covenant?) before discharging the claim.**

How much better it would be if a landlord had some scope for putting itself in the same position as the tenant, with the comfort of knowing it had the ability to walk away, come hell or high water, from its obligations when it came to assign?

Although assuredly not the intention behind the Act (which in itself should give rise to danger signals if – or perhaps more accurately when – the point comes to court), the draftsman might perhaps inadvertently have given the landlord an opportunity for a let-out. The Act specifically allows parties to a tenancy to agree to release their opposite numbers from their covenants (s 26(1)(a)). Why cannot the landlord have included in a new tenancy a clause providing for its release in the stated circumstances?

What does a tenant now have to do to assign?

NB If you are a tenant under a lease of an agricultural holding, a farm business tenancy or under what the Act calls 'a residential lease, namely a lease by which a building or part of a building is let wholly or mainly as a single private residence' (s 22('1E')), the Act does *not* affect you as far as your ability to assign your new tenancy is concerned. You carry on as before which means take advice unless you feel sure you know your way round what tend to be legal minefields in any case.

As a landlord proposing to deal with a 'residential lease', you may well need to take immediate legal advice in any case.

There is yet another pitfall possibly lying in wait for the unwary. The definition of such a lease includes part of a building 'let wholly or mainly as a single private residence'. Obviously, a letting within a multi-occupied block of flats is a 'residential lease' for this purpose but what of a demised building where a small part only is used 'wholly or mainly as a single private residence', perhaps for planning reasons, eg a shop with a small flat above? It is at the least highly arguable that it is also a 'residential lease' within the definition. If so, the landlord of such a property cannot rely on the new rules regarding its ability to control assignments, which may come as something of a nasty shock.

> **Rule 38: parties to a new tenancy must look out for any part of the demise capable of being used as a single private residence only and then consider the implications, preferably before they are committed.**

All other new tenancies are caught by the new rules, *including* building leases for a term of more than 40 years of all properties save those of a suitable agricultural and residential nature excluded from this part of the Act as mentioned above. Since 1927, until the last seven years of that term, the tenant of such a lease could assign without landlord's consent, notwithstanding anything said to the contrary. That oft-forgotten rule has now been abolished for relevant new tenancies (s 22('1D')) but they will, as a result, be caught by the Act's new rules instead.

How does the Act change things?

It all depends. This is the one part of the Act which deliberately gives liberal scope for the relevant parties to decide in each case how matters are to be conducted. For example, they are not obliged to follow the new procedure laid down in the Act; it leaves it open for them to decide what the terms permitting an assignment will be, or including whether the old rule will continue solely to apply.

What is the old rule?

Section 19(1) of the Landlord and Tenant Act 1927 in its original form *imposed an obligation on a landlord to act reasonably when its consent was needed to the assignment* of all leases except agricultural ones. The same inference applies, and *will continue unfettered by the Act to apply*, to any covenant in any such lease providing for landlord's consent to an underletting, charging or parting with possession other than by assignment. We return later to underlettings but note surrenders are not covered.

This rule has been the subject of much consideration in the courts but, whilst they have endeavoured to set down general (and vague) principles governing the way the test of reasonableness should be interpreted, they have made it clear that, subject to these, it is a question of fact in each case as to whether the landlord has acted reasonably. The degree of uncertainty introduced thereby has for many years been a matter of concern to both landlords and tenants. However, the former felt especially frustrated by the courts interpreting attempts to set out in advance the terms upon which consent would be given as breaching the intent behind the rule and, therefore, as invalid.

The result was, in effect, to present landlords with three options when considering how to control the ability of their tenant to transfer his interest. They could, either in whole or in part, (a) impose absolute restrictions on the tenant's ability to deal with his interest, (b) attempt to impose preconditions to the operation of the alienation provisions (viewed by the Court of Appeal in one famous case as a viable option but always treated by landlords and tenants alike with suspicion) or (c) they had to accept the reasonableness test by giving the tenant scope to alienate his interest with its consent. In reality, landlords always have had difficulty in resisting the latter course to a greater or lesser extent. It thus became the minimum usually expected of them that they would permit their tenants to be able to assign the whole of their interest in the lease; the expectations in this direction of the market can perhaps be best seen when it is necessary to assess the detrimental effect on rack rent levels at review of the absence of such flexibility.

Whilst it is true to say that the existence of the tenant's right to assign the whole of his interest, together with at least some degree of flexibility to underlet, has thus become a standard feature, the substantial reduction in new tenancies of the landlord's ability to seek restitution from its original tenant, and any successors, of a breach of covenant by the current tenant through the abolition of the privity of contract rule was always likely to lead to a rethink by landlords of their options.

If s 19(1) had been left unaltered, this reconsideration might have led to a business tenant being restricted to underletting as his only outlet for defraying his obligations onto others, or greater use might have been made of options to break or of surrender through a condition precedent to any alienation right being introduced.

However, there would have been an even stronger temptation on landlords to attempt to alleviate the problem by reducing the length of the term of new tenancies it was prepared to grant, something which might well have altered for good one of the basic features of the commercial lease market in this country which differentiates it from so many overseas, namely its propensity to expect long terms to be granted of up to, say, 25 years in the case of rack rent leases This tendency had already been substantially dissipated by the recession and the concomitant reluctance of tenants, with the market so much in their favour, to commit themselves to lengthy terms without considerable inducement, including a ready supply of break options.

In order no doubt to partly reduce that temptation, those negotiating the compromise which forms the basis of the Act decided, in effect, to remove the common law application of the old rule which led to the landlord to a lease or tenancy not being able safely to predetermine the conditions that a prospective assignee must meet before he could proceed. In this way, that element of uncertainty can now be removed to the extent that the parties agree and, in particular, the landlord is able to introduce such specific controls over, say, the level of covenant strength as it believes it needs or can get away with to protect its investment.

This variation, it should again be stressed, does not remove from the law s 19(1) of the Landlord and Tenant Act 1927 as originally drafted; it amends it where the parties so agree. This explains the quotation marks used in this guide when identifying the parts of s 22 of the Act which deal with the relevant changes; they relate to the extra clauses grafted onto the old sub-s (1).

Indeed, there are some very experienced practitioners, both in the valuation and the legal world, who believe that, for a very good reason as they see it, it will become common in many cases for the landlord to continue to rely virtually alone on the general test of reasonableness, as interpreted over the years in common law, as the main plank for its controlling future assignees, albeit now aided no doubt by a recognition of the change to the test introduced by the landlords' much restricted ability to pursue former tenants and their sureties.

To what extent can the old rule now be amended?

(1) The landlord and the tenant for the time being of the new tenancy can enter into an agreement (whether in the lease itself or not (s 22('1B')) at any time *before* landlord's consent for the assignment in question is applied for, specifying:

(a) the circumstances in which the landlord (and its successors) may withhold its consent; or

(b) the conditions subject to which consent will be given.

If the landlord under the new tenancy then withholds its consent to any such assignment on the ground (and it is the case) that any such circumstances exist or if it gives its consent subject to any such conditions, it shall, respectively, no longer be deemed to be acting unreasonably nor imposing unreasonable conditions (s 22('1A')).

(2) Just by using this ability to predetermine the relevant circumstances or conditions which will govern whether any such consent is to be given and, if so, on what basis does not necessarily prevent the use of a test of reasonableness, albeit it may well be a different one than applicable under the unamended old rule.

Here, it has to be said, the drafting of the Act seems to take on, not for the first time, as we have seen, a degree of opaqueness.

It is of vital importance always to bear in mind that the old test of reasonableness is not dispensed with in an agreement to the extent that any circumstances or conditions specified in it are 'framed by reference to any matter falling to be determined by the landlord *or by any other person'* unless under the agreement's terms:

(a) that person's power to determine that matter is required to be exercised reasonably; *or*

(b) the tenant has 'an *unrestricted* right to have any such determination reviewed by' an independent person whose identity can be ascertained from the agreement and whose decision is stated in it to be *conclusive* (s 22('1C')).

It follows that, if the parties introduce a circumstance or condition into the agreement with any element of discretion in it, eg the circumstance that an assignee must not be of lower financial status than the tenant, the above requirement will have to be followed very carefully if the landlord (or, indeed, the tenant or his surety) is particularly keen to avoid the risk of the old unfettered rule coming into play by the relevant condition being ignored and replaced to the extent necessary by the test of general reasonableness only.

If, on the other hand, specific accounting tests of a purely factual nature were used, eg the net assets or profits of the assignee-to-be (and any sureties) were not less than those of the tenant (or of his sureties, if any) in their respective audited accounts, the objective of a provision that works under the new regime should, on the face of it, be more safely achieved. But, even here – see Example (15) on page 51, there might still be an argument if either the accounting definitions used for the purposes of comparison were capable of different technical interpretation or if they gave rise to different results, depending upon which test you used; can it not then be submitted that the condition is 'framed by reference to a matter falling to be determined by ... [a] person for the purpose of the agreement'(s 22('1C'))?

Efforts have been made, sure enough, to come up with a definitive objective financial test of comparison between existing and proposed covenant strengths (please see Example 16 on page 52) but it is difficult to see the element of subjectivity being entirely eliminated, certainly from the overall equation used in, say Example (6) on page 50. After all, surely, different standards apply to quoted and private companies, let alone to partnerships or other forms of unincorporated entities, and what about economic conditions? The wild swings of fortune engendered by the general economic climate of recent times are surely enough to convince even the most ardent believer in the efficacy of an objective financial test of the dangers, if not impracticality, of excluding wider conditions from consideration in deciding the suitability of a proffered covenant.

Assuming, therefore, that the parties intend to allow at least some element of discretion into the process of deciding whether or not a proposed assignment meets the required tests or standards, the following potential snags need to be borne in mind when considering the appropriate wording:

(i)   The Act identifies two alternative ways or strands of proceeding, ie it introduces a separate test of reasonableness imposed on the party entitled, by virtue of the wording of the relevant clause, to make the decision, whether it be the landlord or someone else, or a third-party determination procedure instigated by the tenant. However, it has to be assumed that they are not meant to be mutually exclusive since, if they were, certain rather obvious courses of action would be removed, eg the introduction by the parties of the tenant's right to have a nominated, independent third party determine whether the landlord's decision was a reasonable one.

Once they are considered as capable of operating together, however, does this not mean that, if the test is expressed by use of the first strand to be the exercise by the third party of its powers of discretion reasonably (s 22 ('1C')(a)), the tenant's right to bring in the third party for a final decision is being fettered, contrary to the strict terms of the second strand proffered under the Act (s ('1C')(b))? Why? Because it is being made open to further review, by a court, as to whether the third party itself has performed reasonably.

(ii) The requirement that the landlord or any other person exercise their powers of discretion reasonably under the new regime seems all too vague. It is generally understood that the intent is clearly to reduce that element of discretion to a consideration of whether the particular term or condition in question is being met, not to question whether that term or condition is itself reasonable, ie, in our earlier example, the need for the assignee (and any surety) to be of no less financial status than the tenant (and its sureties) is not in question, only whether, in deciding not, the landlord has exercised its discretion reasonably.

However, the Act does not go any further which still leaves open to question whether, in deciding the reasonableness of a particular decision, account has to be taken of the particular circumstances and characteristics of the landlord called upon to make that decision. A completely objective set of criteria may show that the decision was unreasonable but if, say, the landlord making the decision was in receivership, there might be overriding special factors which, quite reasonably in those particular circumstances, made it decide the way it did. Which test will apply?

In this situation, if the courts apply the same principles as they did when interpreting how to apply the old unamended rule, the landlord might well feel confident its decision would be upheld but why should not a court take a more objective and stringent view, having regard to the constraints already imposed by the limited nature of the decision required to be made when dealing with a specific issue compared with the general test of reasonableness imposed under the old rule in its original form?

> **Rule 39: until a definitive decision is handed down, extra special drafting is needed when drawing up the specific terms intended to govern the response when an application to assign is made in order to avoid unwanted arguments at that stage.**

(iii) The second alternative also has its own in-built drawback caused by lack of clarity; this has already been alluded to. The Act talks about the tenant's right to have an original decision 'reviewed' by an independent person whose identity is ascertainable from reading the agreement but goes no further than to make it clear the decision of the review is to be conclusive as to the matter in question (s 22('1C')).

Since the Act is silent as to the form of review that can be employed, it would seem that the decision can be left to the parties to specify (or not, as the case may be) but what happens if the third party is required to be an arbitrator? There has always been some form of appeal provided under the Arbitration Acts and that limited right is again confirmed in the provisions of the new Arbitration 'Act' (at the time of publication, yet to receive Royal Assent).

Rule 40: it is difficult to decide which of the two alternatives from the landlord's perspective is presently the safest route to follow when considering draft discretionary terms for an agreement intended to govern the basis upon which future assignments will be permitted. However, subject to case law as it develops, it would seem preferable for a landlord to rely on the requirement for it and any other requisite party to be reasonable when exercising their power of discretion; as we shall shortly see, that is a course of action recommended by a Working Party reporting on this part of the Act on behalf of the Association of British Insurers.

As far as tenants are concerned, caution might lead them to want to mix the two strands together, if feasible, so that they have a specific right of appeal from the sole use of the landlord's or other third party's discretion, despite the obligation on the latter to be reasonable.

However the parties want to play it, in view of the uncertainties in interpreting the Act commented on above, it is even more essential here that sufficiently expert advice is sought as to such provisions.

Is the revised s 29(1) the only statutory provision the parties need to be aware of?

No, it is not.

(1)   The Landlord and Tenant Act 1988 continues to impose duties on a landlord who is required to give consent in accordance with the old reasonableness rule as duly amended by this Act.

Briefly, these duties include:

(a)   to give consent except where it is reasonable not to;

(b)   to give its decision in writing within a reasonable time, with its written reasons for withholding consent or for imposing conditions; and

(c)   to pass on applications to superior landlords where necessary, the latter being placed under similar duties as applicable (see the section on 'Underleases' from page 66).

It is important to note that the 1988 Act *gives a tenant the right to sue in damages* if the landlord was in breach, in effect giving a tenant for the first time an effective remedy to use against a landlord 'unreasonably' withholding consent within that Act's terms; this also continues to be the case.

(2)   Again, where there is a qualified covenant, but where it also provides for obtaining the landlord's consent to an underletting as well as an assignment, it

falls within the ambit of the oft-forgot s 144 of the Law of Property Act 1925. This has the effect of preventing the payment of a fine or sum of money to the landlord (other than reasonable costs and expenses) in respect of its giving consent *unless the lease contains an express provision to the contrary or the parties agree otherwise in the course of negotiating the particular consent.* Will more landlords be tempted to take advantage of this, now ground rules for an assignment can be set out in advance? If they are, they should have an advance look at the anti-avoidance provisions (ss 25(1)(b) and (c)) and then decide, in the light of the later comments on anti-avoidance from page 69 onwards, whether they are still tempted.

The author makes no apology for having taken up so much space in setting out the legal basis upon which the terms relating to the ability to assign will operate in commercial leases, since the changes introduced here come into effect only when the parties to a new tenancy for the time being so decide, unlike the changes introduced by the Act to deal either with the abolition or the amendment of the old law on privity of contract which have to be followed and within which it is assuredly intended the parties must operate.

If it is entirely left to the market to decide whether and how to use this new freedom introduced by the Act, how much more important it is than usual that it should thoroughly understand the legal context in which it must make its decisions and their consequences.

What are the practical consequences of the changes introduced by the Act?

Nobody knows at the inception of the Act's life how things are eventually going to settle down but guidelines will be sought and need to be given. The following is an attempt to assist in this regard as at the date of publication.

Examples of possible circumstances where landlord would become entitled to withhold consent:

(1)   during a specified period of the term to lock in eg

    (a)   the original tenant for the initial period of the term, and/or

    (b)   its successors after they take an assignmen, or

    (c)   during the latter part of the term, to prevent the then tenant from assigning so that he and nobody else is entitled to the security of tenure rights of a business tenant in possession;

(2)   to prevent assignment until the day before the first rent review date so as to avoid such a restriction having an adverse effect on the reviewed rent;

(3) with a new scheme, until the development is let to a specified limit – particularly useful with 'anchor' tenants;

(4) for a particular period to protect tenant mix in a multi-let development;

(5) to prohibit certain uses – this would have to complement the user clause and could be used in conjunction with the term immediately above;

(6) the assignee is not of equivalent [financial] status to the sitting tenant (plus or minus any guarantor?) or other the original tenant – already mentioned when discussing the difficulty of avoiding an element of discretion in the decision process as to whether a test is met;

An example of such a clause is set out below, involving, because aimed at a key retail letting, the overall financial status of the original tenant package:

For the purposes of s 19(1A) of the Landlord and Tenant Act (as amended) it is agreed that the Landlord may withhold its consent to an assignment of the whole of the demised premises where the person to whom the Tenant in whom the Term is vested at the date of the application made by such Tenant for the Landlord's consent to the proposed assignment wishes to assign this Lease ('the Proposed Assignee') is at the date of the said application of materially lesser covenant strength than the guarantor (if any) of the Tenant to whom this Lease was first granted ('the Original Tenant'), or if there is no such guarantor the Original Tenant, was at the date of this Lease (and for this purpose the expression 'covenant strength' shall include but not be limited to past record of payment of rent and other sums due, and performance of covenants and conditions under leases of other premises and historic and reasonable expectations as to future trading performance).

(7) the assignee would reduce [materially?] the value of the landlord's reversion – another example where it might be difficult for landlords to avoid the discretionary element being introduced but, prepared to take that point on board, might well become a popular test amongst them (see the clause identified as Clause 3.3.1 on page 63).

An indication of the way a similar sort of provision might apply, but this time referable especially to premises within an industrial estate, retail park or shopping centre or other larger building or complex, is set out in the following example:

For the purposes of s 19(1A) of the 1927 Act (as amended) it is agreed that the Landlord may withhold its consent to an assignment of the whole of the demised premises ('the Proposed Assignment') where the market value lettability and/or marketability of the Landlord's interest in the [Estate/Park/Centre/building or complex] would be adversely affected [in a material way] by the Proposed Assignment when compared with the position immediately prior to completion of the Proposed Assignment on the assumption (if

not a fact) that the Tenant in whom the Term is vested at the date
of the application for the Landlord's consent to the Proposed
Assignment has complied and is complying with the covenants
on his part and the conditions contained in this Lease and taking
account all relevant circumstances known prior to completion of
the Proposed Assignment.

(8)   whilst there are subsisting breaches of covenant – one more example of a
      provision where it could well be argued an element of discretion is involved;

(9)   material breach of the tenant's repairing covenant at the discretion of an
      independent expert surveyor, perhaps based on his view of what a prudent and
      responsible tenant would do to comply;

(10) breach of the rental or service charge or insurance payment obligations – this
      should at least involve a decision of fact only;

(11) in order to protect good estate management – obviously a subjective test going
      to involve the required measure of reasonableness and/or third-party determi-
      nation if it is to work;

(12) the assignee will be in competition with the anchor tenant – again likely to
      involve the discretionary argument unless drawn up very carefully by the
      landlord, and why should the tenant then accept it?

(13) the assignee would not be regarded as institutionally acceptable – surely also a
      subjective test involving the alternative procedure laid down in the Act. As will
      become clearer later, this test is likely at this stage to be viewed as too vague
      and therefore impractical by the institutions themselves;

(14) the assignee is not a public limited company and/or is not providing a guarantor
      or guarantors that meet criteria as specified etc;

(15) the assignee fails to meet certain specified accountancy criteria, eg net profits
      not less than three times passing rent or net assets not less than ten times the
      same – the implicit dangers of involuntarily straying into a subjective analysis
      of these criteria and whether they have been met have already been noted above
      but, subject to these strictures, below is set out the sort of clause which seems
      to have the best chance of passing the objective test:

For the purposes of s 19(1A) of the Landlord and Tenant Act 1927
(as amended) it is agreed that the Landlord may withhold its consent
to an assignment of the whole of the demised premises where the
party to whom the Tenant in whom the Term is vested at the date
of the application by the said Tenant for the Landlord's consent to
such assignment wishes to assign this Lease as stated in such
application ('the Proposed Assignee') is a public or private body
corporate [or partnership] and (i) its net profits before tax for each
of the three financial years of the Proposed Assignee immediately
preceding the date of such application as shown in the audited

accounts of the Proposed Assignee do not exceed the yearly rent first hereby reserved and at that time payable hereunder by a factor of three or (ii) its net assets as shown in its audited accounts for each of the three financial years of the Proposed Assignee immediately preceding the date of such application do not exceed the said rent by a factor of twenty.

(16) the assignee does not meet some credit agency or rating test, whether by comparison with the assignor, an earlier tenant or a guarantor or not – although, on the face of it, this might look like a factual test, remember that the Act introduces the subjective test requirement for any third party called upon to determine any matter under one of these provisions. Why should Dun & Broadstreet or Standard & Poor be excluded from being subject to appeal and/or being expressly required to be reasonable?

(17) the assignee does not provide requisite information, of which the following are but examples:

  (a) certified copies of the proposed assignee's audited accounts for the three immediately preceding years;

  (b) references from (i) the proposed assignee's bankers confirming that he is considered good for the rent and service charges due under the lease and (ii) at least two people with whom he trades at arm's length confirming that the proposed assignee has always been honest and trustworthy and paid all invoices on time;

  (c) if the proposed assignee is a lessee of other premises, references from at least one of its arm's-length landlords confirming that he has been a satisfactory lessee;

  (d) if the landlord decides it needs all or any of the following material to determine whether any of the stated circumstances of the types outlined earlier exist, it can make written request to have produced:

    (i) a certified copy of the proposed assignee's (or his guarantor's) business plan for the five years immediately preceding the application date which should include projected turnover and profit figures and the expansion and disposal programme for that five-year period plus the source and amount of anticipated funding required to achieve the plan targets;

      NB The landlord should beware a hidden trap here. It does *not* want to give a confidentiality undertaking in the lease as this may well discourage a court permitting its release on a subsequent assignment of its reversion but, by all means, when it requests a business plan, it can agree to include in it a confidentiality undertaking.

    (ii) references from all persons providing or who have agreed to provide finance to the proposed assignee and/or guarantor confirming brief details of the amount of such finance and the terms upon which it is being or is to be provided and that they are unaware of any reason why the requisite party should not be able to comply with those terms;

(iii) a list giving details of all the requisite party's lessors with written authority for the landlord to obtain references from all or any of them.

Examples of conditions that might be attached to the landlord's consent:

(1) the assignor must enter into an Authorised Guarantee Agreement [in the form attached to the lease] (see from page 30 for further discussion on this)

> **Rule 41: remember that there is a substantial body of opinion that believes any guarantor of the assignor cannot be required to provide an AGA, as the new regime provides for such a third-party guarantor's liability to cease when the tenant's liability as such does. It is often the case that a plc offers a shell trading company as tenant backed up by a powerful guarantee from its parent. In allowing such a situation the landlord needs to ensure that it has sufficient control over a future assignment to provide additional comfort beyond the assignor's AGA.**

(2) a rent deposit or rent bond arrangement to cover the assignee's future obligations

> **Rule 42: the rent deposit or other arrangement should now cover a sufficient length of time to accommodate the six-month period for recovery against a guarantor, whether in an AGA or not. The best advice for a landlord must, therefore, be that he goes for a minimum deposit or bond equal to nine months' rent and outgoings. Also he should remember the earlier comments as to the hidden snags that lie behind collateral agreements (see pages 26, 27, 29 and 41).**

(3) such other conditions as are required to deal with the above hurdles to the grant of a consent, eg the provision of necessary third-party guarantees, including any bank guarantee, or further accountancy figures or, even, undertakings as to future performance etc

(4) the payment of the costs of the application (and the payment of any fine or sum of money lawfully imposed by the landlord? – see page 48)

How far should the landlord go and, after it decides, what should the clauses look like?

That this is the *key unknown issue* created by the Act can be seen by the many attempts to try and provide an answer that have already been made since the Act came onto the statute book.

One can presently break down the initial attempts by landlords to deal with this crucial area into three schools of thought, namely:

(1)   The minimalist school

(2)   The maximalist school

(3)   The judicious school

They help identify the range of options open to a landlord when deciding, in the light of the prevailing circumstances, the degree to which it wishes to control the activities of its tenant (or subtenant) when the latter desires to assign.

(1) The minimalist school

Mention has already been made of those that believe restraint should be the first priority amongst landlords when they come to consider the wide cornucopia of options open to them as a result of the changes initiated by the Act. Fully cognisant as they are with 'the double-edged sword', of which more later, they believe that many landlords should rely on the old reasonableness test, fortified, from their standpoint, by the commonly perceived assumption, yet, of course, to be proved, that the courts will, in respect of new tenancies, now lean more towards the landlord in interpreting that test in recognition of the far reduced level of protection the removal of the old privity rules causes. The only provision occasioned by the Act that might well still be included, notwithstanding that to do so must threaten, to some extent, the chances of the above assumption working as the landlord might ideally wish, is the condition that requires the assignor to enter into an Authorised Guarantee Agreement at the landlord's instigation.

To a tenant this is, of the three routes proposed, obviously the one most likely to appeal since there are no specific obstacles to overcome when he comes to assign, and he has the comfort of being faced with a test he knows will not unfairly fetter his ability to alienate his interest; the one specific condition imposed does not affect that ability, it just delays his withdrawal from any liability to the landlord. As is reinforced below, this is something always to be borne in mind by a landlord more concerned with the ability to obtain income from its property than in necessarily ensuring full marketability of the investment it has thereby created.

The suggested wording might be as follows:

> **Not to assign the whole of the demised premises without the prior written consent of the Landlord (such consent not to be unreasonably withheld) provided that the Landlord shall be entitled (for the purposes of s 19(1A) of the Landlord and Tenant Act 1927) to impose as a condition of its consent the execution and delivery to the Landlord prior to the assignment in question of a deed of guarantee (being an authorised guarantee agreement within s 16 of the Landlord and Tenant (Covenants) Act 1995) in the form set out in Schedule [ ] [alternatively in a form reasonably required by the Landlord].**

(2) The maximalist school

There always has been, and no doubt always will be, a school of thought which believes that, whatever the negotiating strength of the prospective parties to an agreement, the best way to approach the task in hand is to put everything bar the kitchen sink into the initial draft of the relevant document in reliance on the age-old maxim that 'nothing ventured is nothing gained'. You will often be regaled by proponents of this tactic with examples of cases when they obtained, more by default than any other conceivable reason, the agreement of the opposition to a document containing large tracts which they would never have dreamed of accepting if they had been acting on the other side.

This leaves aside the more cynical argument that might be put forward in support of such a tactic, namely that you can hardly be accused of negligence, even with the benefit of hindsight, if you endeavour to cover every conceivable line of approach at the inception of the deal.

Whatever the reasoning, the greater room for manoeuvre given by the Act to landlords in appropriate new tenancies has encouraged some to exercise their drafting skills to the full by using many of the extensive range of possible terms available to be imposed by a landlord. Examples of these and of the type of detail and complexity which can be employed in settling them were set out between pages 49 and 53.

Even though the minimalist approach of the general reasonableness test and the ability to require authorised guarantee agreements is likely to form the bedrock of any landlord's approach to this issue, it is again emphasised that a landlord is unlikely to want to insist on the retention of all the other terms set out above. Many of them may be appropriate only to a major letting where the strength of the original tenant's covenant is of great importance to the viability and pricing of the deal. Accordingly, the reader must, it is repeated, carefully consider each clause in the light of the particular transaction being dealt with and also of the remarks that follow.

(3) The judicious approach

You might think that the wide variation of terms that we have now seen can be imposed by landlords in appropriate new tenancies would be giving rise all over the country to them, their agents and solicitors formulating ever-longer lists of requirements to be included in their new deals.

However, whilst consideration of their tactics on how to use the new regime in new tenancies should be a priority amongst landlords and their backers, particularly mortgagees, as well indeed, as their prospective tenants, it is again stressed that the former really should not get carried away with their new freedom by imposing inappropriate conditions. This is so especially, perhaps, when they are being pushed to do so by their funders who, as has been seen, may well have as their priority the need to protect the safety of the income from the mortgaged property as security for the repayment of their loan facility.

For a start, a landlord may well have no need to encompass the whole range of options open to it. After all, as has already been pointed out, there is a huge difference between getting away a letting of a large 'trophy' office building in, say, the City of London from trying to let a secondary retail pitch in a local shopping centre. Whilst the covenant strength of the tenant for the time being in the former case may well be of fundamental, if not overriding, concern to the landlord, it may be the last thing the putative landlord of the latter should be worried about. Even if it does not feel it can be so relaxed as to follow the minimalist approach alone, as outlined earlier, as long as it knows it can also require a rent deposit or bond or bank guarantee, its interest in the status of the actual tenant may well be thereby satisfied.

Apart from the 'horses for courses' argument, the concept of '*the double-edged sword*' mentioned earlier needs to be borne in mind.

This works two ways. First, there is not much point in imposing a list of stringent conditions if the landlord cannot get a tenant to agree them. It has to adopt its strategy for its particular market which, as it becomes adjusted to the new regime, is likely to want the basis by which a prospective tenant can assign to be part of the initial heads-of-terms package; thus, astute landlords concerned with marketing their property in the best manner are increasingly likely, especially in a competitive market, to use the basis through which flexibility of assignment can be given as a marketing weapon. The opportunities for innovative drafting may, as a result, be increased even further but, essentially, no well-advised tenant is going to want to be in a position where he can be held to his commitments for an inordinately lengthy period of time without the necessary ability to pass them on to other parties.

Indeed, the author is aware that, at the time of writing, one of the major covenants in the letting market goes even further. This entity not only insists on obtaining the maximum flexibility to assign but is adamant that it be released forthwith on such assignment from any obligations under the tenant covenants; no AGA for it. Thus, even the minimalist approach exemplified earlier is beyond the pale for this particular prospective tenant.

The other perceived way in which the use of stringent provisions governing assignments can rebound on the landlord only bites once it has managed to get its lease away in a format which, on the face of it, ties down the tenant in severe fashion. However pleased the landlord may feel at having persuaded its tenant to sign up to such a lease, it may only have done so because the tenant has been sufficiently encouraged by the likely downward effect such provisions will have when the time comes to review his rent. Reliant on the principle that the more onerous from usual the tenant's restrictions are the greater the discount he should get on the prevailing market rent at review, leading practitioners of rent reviews have been at pains to highlight the dangers inherent in such an approach, especially whilst old leases remain prevalent in the market as ready comparables.

Some words of reminder to all tenants looking longingly at catching out their landlord on review. Firstly, they have to ensure they do not get caught out by having slipped into the rent review provisions an additional assumption that the standard old-fashioned rule as to assignment on the basis only of landlord's consent not to be unreasonably withheld is to apply to the notional lease being reviewed instead of the tough requirements actually set out in the lease in question.

It could be even more disastrous if they were to allow, as an additional stated factor to be disregarded, any adverse effect on rent of those tough conditions imposed on the tenant plus the disregard itself as well. It may well be true that a landlord required to justify such terms before a court will be faced with an unsympathetic reception but why should a tenant take the chance the court will feel itself to be left with no alternative but to find for the landlord?

Even if they do not succeed in at least muddying the waters in the review provisions, landlords have a counter-argument up their sleeve when comparing old leases with new tenancies. The latter may well make it more difficult for a tenant to assign but such a tenant does not have to worry about privity of contract any more which, even with an obligation to take up an AGA lying around, must be a plus point in comparison and thus, on the same principle, worth an uplift in the rent.

The market should in due course send out signals as to what is regarded as acceptable in the prevailing circumstances, led no doubt, firstly, by the institutions in their perceived role as the ultimate investment purchaser, then by mortgagees in their role as funders and, lastly, by the considered minimum requirements of the letting market without whom, as recent years have clearly emphasised, nothing much can happen anyway. What is likely to be of concern for longer, however, are the drafting points that will be fought over in many deals to come, not least because of the uncertainties interpretation of the Act itself is likely to cause.

With all the above in mind, the efforts of one body, representing as it does so many of the leading institutions, to produce at such an early date in the Act's life, in its words, 'a uniformity of approach to the conditions landlords will seek to include in new leases ... to control assignments' is worthy of detailed attention.

That body, *The Association of British Insurers* (ABI), set up a Working Party with terms of reference as follows:

> To consider and recommend the conditions which should be included in leases to control assignments following the introduction of the Act. To consider possible wordings to be used and the production of model clauses, and to identify the nature and degree of tests to be applied in controlling assignments and to be clear on the grounds upon which landlords could refuse consent to assign.

The members of the Working Party included representatives of such major institutions as the Prudential, Legal and General, Norwich Union and Commercial Union and also to be found were members of major English and Scottish law firms as well as a leading surveyor and accountant.

Between them, they have attempted to meet their original aim. This was to provide a set of provisions capable of producing a uniformity of approach amongst landlords concerned not only to protect the investment value of their assets but also, 'with the adoption of a common standard, to exercise sufficient control of assignments to prevent significant increase in the risks to cash flow, whilst avoiding any adverse impact on rents at review' through the degree of control adopted becoming standard through most modern leases.

Whilst only time will tell as to the extent to which they succeed, in the author's opinion their attempt represents as measured and authoritative approach as is likely to be found anywhere at this date. For this reason, there follows a detailed appraisal of the Report in the hope that its propagation may assist in helping to bring light into a marketplace where there is, at present, plenty of confusion.

Background to ABI Report

With the help of the Report, therefore, it is possible to ascertain the way the Working Party approached their task and, in particular, the nature of the wide range of tests and conditions which they considered, on reflection, should not be adopted for inclusion in their draft clauses.

Two general thoughts of the Working Party in this connection are especially worth noting:

(1) If they were too specific in drawing up the terms and conditions, they believed the courts might infer that those matters which were excluded were of lesser importance to the landlord.

The Report gives examples of specific circumstances where the members clearly took the line of least resistance on the basis that, where the issue was significant, it would in any case be reasonable to refuse consent under the general reasonableness test, based on the old rule, that they have included in their standard terms:

- assignment could not occur where there were material breaches of covenant;

- the tenant had not completed required works;

- there were uncompleted licences or rent reviews outstanding.

The Working Party also pointed out that none of the above cases was directly related to cashflow, the protection of which was one of their basic aims, whilst other factors, including tenant mix or types of user or trading style (which were better controlled in any case in the user provisions), would also be covered under the general reasonableness test.

(2) They concluded it was very difficult to devise a financial test or tests which could apply in the majority of cases.

This, perhaps the most important conclusion they came to, meant that a range of options were rejected. They fell broadly into two categories:

(a) *Financial tests*

These included, they state, gearing tests, operating cashflow, the level of bank facilities and, of course, the profits and net assets tests which are expressly provided for within Example (15) on page 51. However, the Working Party concluded that there was no single test, or combination of tests, which could be applied consistently to produce a reliable result. They pointed out that many entities approaching financial difficulty could pass one or more of the tests whilst, at the same time, many financially sound entities could fail one or more of them. Quoted as an example is even a major clearing bank which failed a three years' profit test!

(b) *Credit Rating test*

These include a reference to an equivalent covenant strength as measured by one of the major credit reference agencies or a minimum credit rating requirement as mentioned in Example (16) on page 52; even there it is required to be treated with caution. The Working Party, for its part, are certainly not impressed; they regard such a measure as crude, backward-looking and open to the result of the landlord being left as its successive tenants with companies of different financial strength but achieving the same credit rating. The upshot, in their opinion, will be that an unsatisfactory covenant could pass the test.

As a consequence of the above, the Working Party fell back, as already mentioned, on the old rule and its concept of general reasonableness which, they pointed out, confers an ability to consider a broad range of factors in coming to a judgment on the suitability of a proposed assignee. They felt that it would give a landlord greater scope to exercise control than very precise and rigid tests.

Even so, there was one further subjective test which the Working Party thought had some merit. This allows a landlord to refuse consent where the value of its reversion will be diminished as a result of the proposed assignment. Obviously, the concern here is that any significant increased risk to the cashflow would normally be reflected in the value of that cashflow. The Working Party's expectation is that a valuer, in considering whether there has been such a reduction, would take into account all the factors affecting the proposed assignee's covenant. However, it was recognised that its application could not be expected to be universal and it would have to be left as an option only.

In particular, the members of the Working Party felt that this provision would be fiercely resisted by High Street multiples and, further, add little benefit to the landlord of large multi-let properties. They thought, more debatably in the writer's opinion, it has to be said, that it would be of larger benefit in more secondary situations where 'the strength of a tenant's covenant is of greater importance than other property factors'. There may well be plenty of times when that is the case but the more the property in question is secondary the less likely, surely, the strength of the covenant will be the top priority and the more the landlord will be concerned with flexibility, both in getting the letting away and giving a doubtful tenant the incentive to assign.

Before turning to the detail of the draft clauses put forward as the framework for inclusion in new leases, mention should be made of other possible terms that were rejected for inclusion as part of the hoped-for new minimum standard for each lease.

Thus, not surprisingly, an absolute bar on assignment was viewed as draconian for this purpose even though the Working Party could see it applied in very particular circumstances. However, it would then, they concede, have a very severe impact on the rent achievable at first letting and at review (unless, of course, it 'disappeared' for latter purposes).

More controversially perhaps, they also regarded as inappropriate for inclusion in every lease a specific requirement for a rent deposit or third-party guarantee. It would be sufficiently reasonable, in their view, to require such additional security as a condition of a particular assignment if the proposed assignee's covenant was not satisfactory. Even so, provision for this specific right as an optional condition to be included in the lease is made in their clauses set out below. There may well be many landlords who, rather than rely on the old rule, will want the comfort of a specific right to call for a rent deposit (or, indeed, bond and/or third-party guarantee) when thought reasonable.

The way the draft clauses are drawn up follows the way that we have seen is provided for in the Act, namely by splitting between circumstances and conditions that will control any granting of consent to an assignment.

Circumstances which allow a landlord to withhold consent include, where the assignee is not of sufficient financial standing to comply with the tenant's obligations under the lease but also where the assignee is an associated company of the tenant.

In this latter case, the intention is to help prevent the movement of assets and liabilities within a group of companies so that the ultimate tenant in possession is a shell with no assets. A point that was noted before, this could well leave the landlord with no worthwhile recourse against an authorised guarantor in the event of default by the assignee that takes over the lease. One word of warning, however. As the Report admits, such tenants usually want some operational flexibility and it is prudent to draft leases so as to permit the sharing of possession within group companies provided no tenancies are created thereby.

Conditions used in the draft clauses to govern the terms upon which consent might be given include, very properly in the author's view, the provision in each and every case of an authorised guarantee and prior payment of all sums due under the lease.

Lastly, as background, mention is appositely made in the Report of the need not to read alienation provisions in isolation from the rest of the lease. As representatives of the interests of institutions, therefore, the Working Party assume that the remainder of the lease will be drafted in the appropriate modern form to allow landlords to exercise sufficient control over the tenant's occupation of the demise.

ABI's draft clauses and commentary

Please note:

(1) The commentary that accompanies the clauses is meant to be read together with these preliminary notes when considering the inclusion of such conditions and circumstances in the new tenancy under contemplation.

(2) A few areas within the drafting (eg paragraphs 2 and 3 of Option 1) have deliberately been dealt with in 'shorthand' as each landlord will no doubt have its preferred wording.

(3) Where the lease in question is a sublease, the terms of the superior lease (in particular those relating to assignments of subleases) will, of course, need to be borne in mind when framing the alienation clauses. In this context paragraph 1 of Option II of the draft clauses below may be relevant and the remarks concerning Underleases that commence on page 66 certainly are.

(4) The ABI draft clauses do not provide for any reference to an independent third-party determination. The Working Party decided that 'for the sake of simplicity, and to limit the possibility of a two tier approach, the services of the court are relied on' where the exercise of some element of discretion has to be capable of being tested for reasonableness.

Remember the warning signalled earlier on page 47, to the effect that using an arbitrator to determine the issue might be construed as capable of leading to a breach of the requirement that the third party's determination be conclusive. Even though referral to an expert, rather than an arbitrator, would get round that problem, Rule 40 agrees with the ABI, on balance, that it may be safer, at least during the Act's early days, for the landlord to rely on the courts determining an argument over the exercise of the landlord's discretion rather than such a third-party expert.

(5) The ABI suggests that a landlord may wish to draft the surety provision so that the surety also guarantees the tenant's obligations under an AGA. Before taking up this suggestion, however, the reader should bear in mind the comments earlier as to this subject on pages 31 and 32 which highlight the real difficulty in assuming the surety can be put under a binding obligation to enter into an AGA once the tenant in question has assigned.

Working draft clauses (with commentary)

1 Not to assign the whole of the demised premises without the prior written consent of the Landlord (such consent not to be unreasonably withheld) provided that the Landlord shall be entitled (for the purposes of s 19(1A) of the Landlord and Tenant Act 1927):

1.1 to withhold its consent in any of the circumstances set out in Clause 3;

1.2 to impose all or any of the matters set out in Clause 4 as a condition of its consent.

2 The provisos to Clause 1 shall operate without prejudice to the right of the Landlord to withhold such consent on any other ground or grounds where such withholding of consent would be reasonable or to impose any further condition or conditions upon the grant of consent where the imposition of such condition or conditions would be reasonable.

(**NB** In the author's opinion, the need for this Clause 2 is not obvious. Clause 1 appears to have been very carefully drafted to stay within the framework laid down in the Act for validly including provisions for specific circumstances and conditions so that the old general reasonableness rule remains in any event. It might have been more relevant if Clause 2 had instead made it clear that this general test of reasonableness must have due regard to the introduction of the Act and its particular effect in the case of the lease in question.)

3 The *circumstances* referred to in Clause 1.1 above are as follows:

3.1 Where the assignee is an associated company of the Tenant.

The reasoning behind this clause was explained earlier. The Working Party points out that the lease will have to specify a definition of 'associated company' and, in return for obtaining an agreement from a tenant to its inclusion, may need to provide for increased sharing of possession among associated companies.

There are a lot of landlords that are nervous about agreeing the last point and for them the ABI sets out the following fall-back positions:

(a) to provide for the lease to be assigned to the assignee jointly with the existing associated tenant or with the parent company. In the light of the ostensibly draconian anti-avoidance provisions of the Act, care will have to be taken to ensure this is not open to attack.

(b) the landlord makes no special provision for intergroup assignments and the parties rely on 'the sufficient financial standing' test, ie Clause 3.2 below.

(c) the landlord might take up the option of an 'equivalent status' clause as set out in paragraph 1 of Option I below but applicable to intergroup assignments only. The Working Party go on to suggest this could be further qualified as follows:

   (i) where another associated or group company assignee fails the 'equivalent status' test, the lease could still allow the assignment to proceed as long as another associated or group company, this time of equivalent status to the assignor, guarantees the obligations of the assignee; but

(ii) the new associated or group company guarantor could also guarantee the obligations of any further assignee that is an associated or group company. However, remember this might not be allowed under the Act.

3.2 Where in the reasonable opinion of the Landlord the proposed assignee is not of sufficient financial standing to enable it to comply with the tenant's covenants in the Lease.

We are reminded that the use of the word 'reasonable' makes this clause susceptible to review by the court.

[Additional optional circumstances are set out below as:

Option 1

3.3.1 Where in the reasonable opinion of the Landlord the value of the Landlord's interest in the demised premises would be diminished or otherwise adversely affected by the proposed assignment on the assumption (whether or not a fact) that the Landlord wished to sell its interest the day following completion of the assignment of this Lease to the proposed assignee.

It has already been pointed out that the Working Party believed this, the 'equivalent status' test, may be unacceptable to many a major retailer; they have thus included it as an option only. In particular, the Report alludes to the fact that the diminution of value covered in the clause could just as well also touch on the landlord's reversion to the building or centre of which the demised premises might form but part. In this respect, nevertheless, a landlord may still be tempted by the type of clause set out in Example 7 on page 50 if it thought the circumstances warranted it.

3.3.2 Where the proposed assignee enjoys diplomatic or state immunity [but this circumstance shall not apply where the proposed assignee is the Government of the United Kingdom of Great Britain and Northern Ireland or any department thereof].

3.3.3 Where the proposed assignee is not resident [in the United Kingdom of Great Britain and Northern Ireland] [in the EC] [in a jurisdiction where reciprocal enforcement of judgments exists].

The concepts outlined above will, says the Working Party, need more elaborate definition depending on the landlord's precise concerns They suggest that, in the case of a corporation, the location of its registered office might be the most relevant factor. Whatever test is used, care needs to be taken in the drafting. Too narrow a requirement might adversely affect the rent.]

4 The conditions referred to in clause 1.2 are as follows:

4.1 The execution and delivery to the Landlord prior to the assignment in question of a deed of guarantee (being an authorised guarantee agreement within s 16 of the Landlord and Tenant (Covenants) Act 1995 [in the form set out in Schedule [ ] [in a form reasonably required by the Landlord].

Each landlord, the Report says, will probably end up with its own preferred form of AGA. As it points out, an AGA can largely follow the terms of the usual type of third-party guarantee subject, of course, to the parameters set out in the Act; in particular the guarantor's liability as the earlier tenant under an AGA must end on a lawful assignment by the assignee he was guaranteeing. Whether a requirement that any guarantor of such a party when the tenant in possession must also enter into the AGA is valid is, as we have seen, unclear.

4.2 The payment to the Landlord of all rents and other sums which have fallen due under the Lease prior to the date of the assignment.

It has already been seen that the members of the Working Party did not feel it necessary to make it a specific requirement that there be no breach of a material nature of *any* substantive covenant by the tenant as a condition to an assignment. They clearly felt it sufficient to cover specifically payment of monies under the lease only on the grounds that any other significant breach could be a reason for the landlord reasonably refusing under the old rule as provided for in Clause 1 above.

[Other optional conditions are set out below as:

Option 2

4.3.1 The assignment shall not take place until any requisite consent of any superior landlord or mortgagee has been obtained and any lawfully imposed condition of such consent satisfied.

The valid point is made in the Report that, depending on the terms of the superior lease or any mortgage in question, this clause could render the lease unassignable and, if not, could at least be construed as very restrictive. Landlords should, therefore, consider carefully the terms of any superior lease or mortgage, in so far as the former is concerned, also in the light of what is shortly to follow. ·

4.3.2 The execution and delivery to the Landlord prior to the assignment of a rent deposit deed for such sum as the Landlord may reasonably determine in the form set out in Schedule [ ] [or in such form as the Landlord may reasonably require]

together with the payment by way of cleared funds of the sum specified in the rent deposit deed.

Reminder is made of the view of the Working Party expressed earlier to the effect that they believed the inclusion of this specific requirement to be unnecessary as the landlord could rely on the general rule to support it when the covenant offered was unsatisfactory. It was prudent of them, however, to include this clause as an optional extra as there are many landlords who will want the assurance of its inclusion irrespective of any perceived effect on rent review.]

Where to now?

As to how the market might go, there are, as can be gleaned from the comments above on the wide range of possible options for the putative draftsman to consider, already many opinions but the following might be viewed with especial interest:

* more turnover deals to avoid the traditional market rent review, but landlords should remember the possible effect that the involuntary grant of an overriding lease might have (see pages 18 and 19); and

* despite attempts to reverse the trend, an increased tendency to move to shorter leases which will allow the landlord greater freedom to impose stringent terms, if assignment is to be permitted at all, whilst, at the same time, still giving the tenant the ability to decide whether or not to walk away commensurate with the ability to break he might otherwise have had – the possible complication here is the effect of the lease renewal provisions of the 1954 Act, of which more shortly.

> **Rule 43: in the absence of experience as to how markets will settle down in the face of the new regime, from all that has been stated on this issue, the following is offered in the hope that it may be of some assistance to landlords:**

(i) **always go for the right to require an AGA (but even then this may meet resistance from covenants of major strength);**

(ii) **introduce the bare minimum of circumstances that must appertain before consent to an assignment can be entertained;**

(iii) **where of material importance to the deal, concentrate thereby on protecting covenant strength unless particular circumstances call for different priorities, eg protecting tenant mix or alternative uses;**

(iv) **insert the right to require rent deposits and, it is suggested, guarantors unless really concerned as to the possible effect on rent review; and**

(v) **always include a general sweeping-up provision giving discretion based on the old rule to the landlord.**

Part III: Last but not least

Underleases

One option open to a landlord anxious to retain the continued liability of the tenant to whom it originally contracts to give a new tenancy is to heavily restrict his ability to assign but enable him to defray the consequent responsibility through subletting.

So far as commercial property is concerned, it is rare to find situations where the landlord is prepared to give up all control over how its tenant can sublet. Apart from legitimate ongoing management concerns it may have when dealing with, say, a shopping centre or large office building, it must always remain uppermost in its mind that, in due course, it may well inherit such subtenants as its direct tenants if and when they become entitled to new leases as 'occupiers' for the purposes of Part II of the Landlord and Tenant Act 1954.

Indeed, the importance in the case of business tenancies of having some say in who 'occupies' the demise has just been accentuated by the decision of the House of Lords in *Graysim Holdings Ltd v P&O Property Holdings Ltd* [1996] 03 EG 124. There the head landlord of a market which it had let to a market operator was held entitled under the Act to take over the rents of the stallholders when their subleases fell in because the operator failed to have sufficient control of his demise for the purposes of the 1954 Act. One can envisage not only market operators having problems with this decision but also such businesses as the operators of furnished flats and serviced offices having to review their position very carefully.

For those landlords anxious as a result to minimise the opportunity of being faced at the expiry of their headlease with an unwanted new tenant with rights to a new lease, but not having an absolute right to bar the creation of sublettings amongst the tenant covenants, there may still be hope. One obvious answer is to avoid the temptation of serving default notices wherever possible, but likely to be of greater comfort is to remember the ability given to the parties to exclude by agreement, supported by the court, the 1954 Act's security of tenure provisions.

When it comes to seeing how the Act we are dealing with copes with the new situation landlords now find themselves in when granting new tenancies, there appears, for not entirely clear reasons, to be a dichotomy between the position adopted when the tenant first wishes to grant a sublease and that when the subtenant wants to assign.

As pointed out earlier, the new procedures relating to alienation by the tenant do not affect the grant of subleases. So, where consent is needed from the tenant's landlord to his subletting, the tenant can rely upon it being implicit, if the lease does not say so, that the landlord cannot unreasonably withhold consent as understood under the unchanged old rule. Further, remember the relevant terms of the Landlord and Tenant Act 1988 as set out in para (1) on page 48.

However, there appears to be no reason why the changes introduced by the Act to the old rule cannot touch the assignment of any interest, whether of whole or part, in the premises so demised (s 22('1E')(a)), including, therefore, that proposed by a sublessor, ie the landlord can ask his tenant legitimately for a prior agreement regulating the precise basis upon which assignments of subleases can take place.

In reality, attempts have often been made in old leases to introduce conditions which must be met in any permitted subletting, eg that it will be in a set form or that the sublessee will give direct covenants operating for the term granted to him, plus guarantees if requested, to the landlord. However, such conditions were, at best, suspect and the changes introduced by the Act are going to make their use in new tenancies even more risky. In any event, the new structure governing the length of liability of tenants under covenants they give seems undoubtedly to embrace subtenants obligating themselves to their superior landlord so that, in most cases, subject only to the AGA rule, they are off the hook once they have assigned.

> **Rule 44: if the landlord has been unable to prevent in suitable terms the tenant granting subleases, whatever else it does to try and control them, any assignment by a subtenant, including the original, should be subject to an AGA being given or, even better, should only be allowed if the assignee as a business tenant agrees to exclude his security of tenure rights.**
>
> **If, however, the landlord wants even greater control over the initial grant of the sublease than permitted under the old rule and is prepared to take a chance on wording in the lease intended to give it such control, the parties should remember that the rule in the 1988 Act entitling the tenant to sue in damages for the loss it may suffer for the landlord's alleged unreasonableness will apply.**

Renewal of business tenancies

Amongst consequential amendments to other legislation caused by the Act's introduction are amendments to Part II of the Landlord and Tenant Act 1954 which, as mentioned above, deals with the security of tenure rights of business tenants. These amendments are important since, for the first time, when considering the terms of the new tenancy to be granted to such a tenant, they require the courts to take into account the provisions of a specific piece of legislation.

The amendments are twofold, involving:

(a) Terms of the new tenancy (other than duration and rent)

In determining these up to now, all the courts have been required by the legislation to do is 'have regard to the terms of the current tenancy and to all relevant circumstances'. Thus, whilst it is not the intention to ossify the provisions so that they must repeat what was in the old lease, the onus is on the party seeking to depart from those terms to show that it is justified as well as reasonable to do so.

Now, when the courts are considering such terms, they are specifically required to include in their consideration of 'all relevant circumstances' the operation of the provisions of the Act (Schedule 1, para 4). It seems clear from this that leases are henceforth going to be reviewed by the courts on the basis not only that privity of contract no longer applies but also that the lease should contain such of the mechanisms introduced by the Act as are deemed necessary to provide the consequent degree of fairness between the parties.

Obviously, the point is likely to be especially contentious when dealing, as initially will happen most of the time, with the renewal of old leases under the new regime. Until matters settle down, how courts will, in particular, deal with requests to include provisions regulating by prior agreement the manner in which assignments will be dealt with remains conjectural. If a landlord asks for an extensive range of conditions, it should not be surprised to find itself being given a hard time if they are thought unfairly to fetter the tenant. On the other hand, the inclusion of a reasonable provision which benefits solely the landlord ought not to be rejected if it is one that will not disadvantage the tenant provided his proffered assignee acts properly as tenant, eg the requirement to provide an AGA.

> **Rule 45: it might be wise for landlords to restrict themselves to the standard conditions listed by the ABI's Working Party plus such of their optional clauses as they consider just and reasonable in the circumstances of the case, at least until the market settles down. When it does, a court may tend to rely on expert evidence of normal practice as the best guide as to what is reasonable in particular circumstances. Also, the parties should always bear in mind that whatever terms are included in the new lease to accommodate the new Act will be borne in mind when the court considers the next item:**

(b) Rent terms

The rent is assessed by the court after the duration and other terms of the new tenancy have been agreed or determined by the court. There are a number of factors that are disregarded but, subject to these, the rent is to be what, 'having regard to the terms of the tenancy (other than those relating to rent), the holding might reasonably be expected to be let in the open market by a willing lessor'.

To this calculation must now be added consideration of 'any effect on rent of the operation' of the Act's provisions (Schedule 1, para 3). This not only includes the effect that assignment provisions introduced as a result of the Act will have on rent but also, probably to balance this, the consequences of the removal of the net benefit the landlord will assuredly claim it gained under the old privity of contract regime.

These factors are, no doubt even more than the nature of the lease's other terms, going to be the province of expert evidence which is likely, at least in respect of the Act's effect on rent for a new tenancy compared with an old lease, to mirror the views taken in commensurate rent review situations, as to which you are referred to the relevant comments on page 23.

> **Rule 46: most lease renewal negotiations are settled before any court hearing, perhaps mainly because the parties are reluctant to place their fate in the hands of a judge to decide the appropriate rent level. This is not, as they would be the first to admit, an area where judges would hold themselves out as having any special level of expertise and how they might interpret the expert evidence placed before them as to the appropriate open market level has, therefore, always been seen as a particularly risky exercise to try and assess in advance. Now that there is a further exercise of rent assessment for them to carry out if called upon, the advice to agree, rather than allow the court to determine, the rent level for the new lease is accentuated.**

Anti-avoidance

On the face of it, the clause in the Act making void any attempt to get round its provisions is so widely worded as to make it look impossible to circumvent (s 25). Indeed, the draftsman felt impelled to provide that it was not meant to stop an AGA (s 25(3)) nor the fact that a covenant is used to prohibit or restrict an assignment or parting with possession (s 25(2)(b)).

Any agreement relating to a tenancy is stated to be void to the extent that it purports to *exclude, modify or otherwise frustrate* the operation of any part of the Act (s 25(1)(a)).

Further, it is also void if it makes provision for the termination or surrender of the tenancy (s 25(1)(b)(i)) or the imposition of any penalty, disability or liability when any part of the Act is operative (s 25(1)(b)(ii)). The Act goes to some length to make it clear that none of these terms can be used in relation in any way to the operation of any provision of the Act (ss 25(1)(b) and (c)), including to the extent that they purport to regulate the giving of, and an application for, consent to an assignment.

With this in mind, you are asked to revisit s 144 of the Law of Property Act 1925 (please turn to para (2) on page 48 and 49 if you need a quick reminder) and review whether you can still include, in a clause regulating the way in which consent to an assignment is dealt with, provision for the tenant to pay up in return for getting that consent.

Notwithstanding all the above, the draftsmen behind the Act seem almost anxious to maintain the air of ambiguity and ambivalence that the author has endeavoured to show permeates so many aspects of the Act. Having taken such great care to try and ensure the structures and mechanisms created by the Act remain inviolate, a further piece of what looks like armour plating is added on, seemingly as an afterthought, just to make doubly sure there is no way to avoid the Act. However, read for yourself the wording in question so that you can form your own view of whether, if this was the objective, it has been achieved:

> This section [ie the anti-avoidance section] applies to an agreement relating to a tenancy whether or not the agreement is:
>
> (a) contained in the instrument creating the tenancy; or
>
> (b) made before the creation of the tenancy (s 25(4)).

No mention is made of 'an agreement' entered into after the tenancy has been created despite, it would seem, that being just as much a possibility as one made before, and the ease with which the words 'or after' could have been added in subclause (b) after the word 'before'. After all, large parts of the Act are taken up with events that happen after a tenancy has been created, eg overriding leases, an AGA or a lease variation itself. Further, the 'agreement' specifying the manner in which assignments are dealt with is expressly stated to apply 'at the time when the lease is granted or at any other time' until application is made for landlord's consent (s 22('1B')(b)). Why could not the point have been covered just as easily here as well?

Perhaps the draftsman thought it unnecessary. The anti-avoidance section does start by stating that 'any agreement relating to a tenancy is void ...' (s 25(1)(i)(a)). Did they think that was enough? In any event, it will, no doubt, also be argued against any attempt to negate the anti-avoidance provisions in this way that, to allow this to happen, would suborn the whole intent behind that section of the Act.

It seems only right to end this guide on a suitably mysterious note but the number of possible difficulties that the author has endeavoured to point out when it comes to the implementation of the Act, let alone many that others are no doubt thinking about, seems destined to keep property litigation lawyers busy for some time to come.

Rule 47: this is not strictly a rule, and certainly should not be construed as advice, but a landlord of a new tenancy in the future, sufficiently concerned about the perceived limitations imposed on it by the Act, might be prepared to go for short leases with no alienation allowed to the tenant but with an agreement entered at the appropriate time extending the term, say, in return for some continuing warranty from that tenant, notwithstanding the number of permitted assignments.

Landlords of an old lease or in relation to an AGA of a new tenancy might feel even more tempted to try this on if, say, their six-month limit for recovery has expired and they can persuade the claimant to agree to an extension since, if declared void, a suitable arrangement could well leave them not that much worse off than they were before.

Finally, there follows a fully-fledged Rule. The moral of the above and much else in this guide is:

YOU WILL NEED TO ENSURE YOU ARE KEPT FULLY UP TO DATE WITH THE CASE LAW ON THE ACT AS IT INEVITABLY DEVELOPS OVER THE COMING YEARS.

Appendix I

Landlord and Tenant (Covenants) Act 1995

CHAPTER 30

ARRANGEMENT OF SECTIONS

ELIZABETH II

Landlord and Tenant (Covenants) Act 1995

1995 CHAPTER 30

An Act to make provision for persons bound by covenants of a tenancy to be released from such covenants on the assignment of the tenancy, and to make other provision with respect to rights and liabilities arising under such covenants; to restrict in certain circumstances the operation of rights of re-entry, forfeiture and disclaimer; and for connected purposes. [19 July 1995]

B E IT ENACTED by the Queen's most Excellent Majesty, by and with the advice and consent of the Lords Spiritual and Temporal, and Commons, in this present Parliament assembled, and by the authority of the same, as follows:—

Preliminary

1.—(1) Sections 3 to 16 and 21 apply only to new tenancies.

(2) Sections 17 to 20 apply to both new and other tenancies.

Tenancies to which the Act applies.

(3) For the purposes of this section a tenancy is a new tenancy if it is granted on or after the date on which this Act comes into force otherwise than in pursuance of—

    (a) an agreement entered into before that date, or

    (b) an order of a court made before that date.

(4) Subsection (3) has effect subject to Section 20(1) in the case of overriding leases granted under Section 19.

(5) Without prejudice to the generality of Subsection (3), that subsection applies to the grant of a tenancy where by virtue of any variation of a tenancy there is a deemed surrender and re-grant as it applies to any other grant of a tenancy.

(6) Where a tenancy granted on or after the date on which this Act comes into force is so granted in pursuance of an option granted before that date, the tenancy shall be regarded for the purposes of Subsection (3) as granted in pursuance of an agreement entered into before that date (and accordingly is not a new tenancy), whether or not the option was exercised before that date.

(7) In Subsection (6) 'option' includes right of first refusal.

2.—(1) This Act applies to a landlord covenant or a tenant covenant of a tenancy—

    (a) whether or not the covenant has reference to the subject matter of the tenancy, and

    (b) whether the covenant is express, implied or imposed by law,

but does not apply to a covenant falling within Subsection (2).

(2) Nothing in this Act affects any covenant imposed in pursuance of—

    (a) Section 35 or 155 of the Housing Act 1985 (covenants for repayment of discount on early disposals);

    (b) paragraph 1 of Schedule 6A to that Act (covenants requiring redemption of landlord's share); or

    (c) paragraph 1 or 3 of Schedule 2 to the Housing Associations Act 1985 (covenants for repayment of discount on early disposals or for restricting disposals).

Transmission of covenants

3.—(1) The benefit and burden of all landlord and tenant covenants of a tenancy—

    (a) shall be annexed and incident to the whole, and to each and every part, of the premises demised by the tenancy and of the reversion in them, and

    (b) shall in accordance with this section pass on an assignment of the whole or any part of those premises or of the reversion in them.

(2) Where the assignment is by the tenant under the tenancy, then as from the assignment the assignee—

    (a) becomes bound by the tenant covenants of the tenancy except to the extent that—

        (i) immediately before the assignment they did not bind the assignor, or

        (ii) they fall to be complied with in relation to any demised premises not comprised in the assignment; and

    (b) becomes entitled to the benefit of the landlord covenants of the tenancy except to the extent that they fall to be complied with in relation to any such premises.

(3) Where the assignment is by the landlord under the tenancy, then as from the assignment the assignee—

    (a) becomes bound by the landlord covenants of the tenancy except to the extent that—

        (i) immediately before the assignment they did not bind the assignor, or

        (ii) they fall to be complied with in relation to any demised premises not comprised in the assignment; and

(b) becomes entitled to the benefit of the tenant covenants of the tenancy except to the extent that they fall to be complied with in relation to any such premises.

(4) In determining for the purposes of Subsection (2) or (3) whether any covenant bound the assignor immediately before the assignment, any waiver or release of the covenant which (in whatever terms) is expressed to be personal to the assignor shall be disregarded.

(5) Any landlord or tenant covenant of a tenancy which is restrictive of the user of land shall, as well as being capable of enforcement against an assignee, be capable of being enforced against any other person who is the owner or occupier of any demised premises to which the covenant relates, even though there is no express provision in the tenancy to that effect.

(6) Nothing in this section shall operate—

(a) in the case of a covenant which (in whatever terms) is expressed to be personal to any person, to make the covenant enforceable by or (as the case may be) against any other person; or

(b) to make a covenant enforceable against any person if, apart from this section, it would not be enforceable against him by reason of its not having been registered under the Land Registration Act 1925 or the Land Charges Act 1972.

(7) To the extent that there remains in force any rule of law by virtue of which the burden of a covenant whose subject matter is not in existence at the time when it is made does not run with the land affected unless the covenantor covenants on behalf of himself and his assigns, that rule of law is hereby abolished in relation to tenancies.

1925 c. 21.
1972 c. 61.

4. The benefit of a landlord's right of re-entry under a tenancy—

(a) shall be annexed and incident to the whole, and to each and every part, of the reversion in the premises demised by the tenancy, and

(b) shall pass on an assignment of the whole or any part of the reversion in those premises.

Transmission of the rights of re-entry.

Release of covenants on assignment

5.—(1) This section applies where a tenant assigns premises demised to him under a tenancy.

(2) If the tenant assigns the whole of the premises demised to him, he—

Tenant released from covenants on assignment of tenancy.

(a) is released from the tenant covenants of the tenancy, and

(b) ceases to be entitled to the benefit of the landlord covenants of the tenancy, as from the assignment.

(3) If the tenant assigns part only of the premises demised to him, then as from the assignment he—

(a) is released from the tenant covenants of the tenancy, and

(b) ceases to be entitled to the benefit of the landlord covenants of the tenancy, only to the extent that those covenants fall to be complied with in relation to that part of the demised premises.

(4) This section applies as mentioned in Subsection (1) whether or not the tenant is tenant of the whole of the premises comprised in the tenancy.

6.—(1) This section applies where a landlord assigns the reversion in premises of which he is the landlord under a tenancy.

Landlord may be released from covenants on assignment of reversion.

(2) If the landlord assigns the reversion in the whole of the premises of which he is the landlord—

(a) he may apply to be released from the landlord covenants of the tenancy in accordance with Section 8; and

(b) if he is so released from all of those covenants, he ceases to be entitled to the benefit of the tenant covenants of the tenancy as from the assignment.

(3) If the landlord assigns the reversion in part only of the premises of which he is the landlord—

(a) he may apply to be so released from the landlord covenants of the tenancy to the extent that they fall to be complied with in relation to that part of those premises; and

(b) if he is, to that extent, so released from all of those covenants, then as from the assignment he ceases to be entitled to the benefit of the tenant covenants only to the extent that they fall to be complied with in relation to that part of those premises.

(4) This section applies as mentioned in Subsection (1) whether or not the landlord is landlord of the whole of the premises comprised in the tenancy.

7.—(1) This section applies where—

(a) a landlord assigns the reversion in premises of which he is the landlord under a tenancy, and

Former landlord may be released from covenants on assigment of reversion.

(b) immediately before the assignment a former landlord of the premises remains bound by a landlord covenant of the tenancy ('the relevant covenant').

(2) If immediately before the assignment the former landlord does not remain the landlord of any other premises demised by the tenancy, he may apply to be released from the relevant covenant in accordance with Section 8.

(3) In any other case the former landlord may apply to be so released from the relevant covenant to the extent that it falls to be complied with in relation to any premises comprised in the assignment.

(4) If the former landlord is so released from every landlord covenant by which he remained bound immediately before the assignment, he ceases to be entitled to the benefit of the tenant covenants of the tenancy.

(5) If the former landlord is so released from every such landlord covenant to the extent that it falls to be complied with in relation to any premises comprised in the assignment, he ceases to be entitled to the benefit of the tenant covenants of the tenancy to the extent that they fall to be so complied with.

(6) This section applies as mentioned in Subsection (1)—

(a) whether or not the landlord making the assignment is landlord of the whole of the premises comprised in the tenancy; and

(b) whether or not the former landlord has previously applied (whether under Section 6 or this section) to be released from the relevant covenant.

8.—(1) For the purposes of Section 6 or 7 an application for the release of a covenant to any extent is made by serving on the tenant, either before or within the period of four weeks beginning with the date of the assignment in question, a notice informing him of—

Procedure for seeking release from a covenant under Section 6 or 7.

(a) the proposed assignment or (as the case may be) the fact that the assignment has taken place, and

(b) the request for the covenant to be released to that extent.

(2) Where an application for the release of a covenant is made in accordance with Subsection (1), the covenant is released to the extent mentioned in the notice if—

(a) the tenant does not, within the period of four weeks beginning with the day on which the notice is served, serve on the landlord or former landlord a notice in writing objecting to the release, or

(b) the tenant does so serve such a notice but the court, on the application of the landlord or former landlord, makes a declaration that it is reasonable for the covenant to be so released, or

(c) the tenant serves on the landlord or former landlord a notice in writing consenting to the release and, if he has previously served a notice objecting to it, stating that that notice is withdrawn.

(3) Any release from a covenant in accordance with this section shall be regarded as occurring at the time when the assignment in question takes place.

(4) In this section—

(a) 'the tenant' means the tenant of the premises comprised in the assignment in question (or, if different parts of those premises are held under the tenancy by different tenants, each of those tenants);

(b) any reference to the landlord or the former landlord is a reference to the landlord referred to in Section 6 or the former landlord referred to in Section 7, as the case may be; and

(c) 'the court' means a county court.

Apportionment of liability between assignor and assignee

9.—(1) This section applies where—

(a) a tenant assigns part only of the premises demised to him by a tenancy;

(b) after the assignment both the tenant and his assignee are to be bound by a non-attributable tenant covenant of the tenancy; and

(c) the tenant and his assignee agree that as from the assignment liability under the covenant is to be apportioned between them in such manner as is specified in the agreement.

(2) This section also applies where—

(a) a landlord assigns the reversion in part only of the premises of which he is the landlord under a tenancy;

(b) after the assignment both the landlord and his assignee are to be bound by a non-attributable landlord covenant of the tenancy; and

(c) the landlord and his assignee agree that as from the assignment liability under the covenant is to be apportioned between them in such manner as is specified in the agreement.

(3) Any such agreement as is mentioned in Subsection (1) or (2) may apportion liability in such a way that a party to the agreement is exonerated from all liability under a covenant.

(4) In any case falling within Subsection (1) or (2) the parties to the agreement may apply for the apportionment to become binding on the appropriate person in accordance with Section 10.

(5) In any such case the parties to the agreement may also apply for the apportionment to become binding on any person (other than the appropriate person) who is for the time being entitled to enforce the covenant in question; and Section 10 shall apply in relation to such an application as it applies in relation to an application made with respect to the appropriate person.

(6) For the purposes of this section a covenant is, in relation to an assignment, a 'non-attributable' covenant if it does not fall to be complied with in relation to any premises comprised in the assignment.

(7) In this section 'the appropriate person' means either—

(a) the landlord of the entire premises referred to in Subsection (1)(a) (or, if different parts of those premises are held under the tenancy by different landlords, each of those landlords), or

(b) the tenant of the entire premises referred to in Subsection (2)(a) (or, if different parts of those premises are held under the tenancy by different tenants, each of those tenants),

depending on whether the agreement in question falls within Subsection (1) or Subsection (2).

10.—(1) For the purposes of Section 9 the parties to an agreement

Apportionment of liability under covenants binding both assignor and assignee of tenancy or reversion.

falling within Subsection (1) or (2) of that section apply for an apportionment to become binding on the appropriate person if, either before or within the period of four weeks beginning with the date of the assignment in question, they serve on that person a notice informing him of—

Procedure for making apportionment bind other party to lease.

(a) the proposed assignment or (as the case may be) the fact that the assignment has taken place;

(b) the prescribed particulars of the agreement; and

(c) their request that the apportionment should become binding on him.

(2) Where an application for an apportionment to become binding has been made in accordance with subsection (1), the apportionment becomes binding on the appropriate person if—

(a) he does not, within the period of four weeks beginning with the day on which the notice is served under Subsection (1), serve on the parties to the agreement a notice in writing objecting to the apportionment becoming binding on him, or

(b) he does so serve such a notice but the court, on the application of the parties to the agreement, makes a declaration that it is reasonable for the apportionment to become binding on him, or

(c) he serves on the parties to the agreement a notice in writing consenting to the apportionment becoming binding on him and, if he has previously served a notice objecting thereto, stating that that notice is withdrawn.

(3) Where any apportionment becomes binding in accordance with this section, this shall be regarded as occurring at the time when the assignment in question takes place.

(4) In this section—

'the appropriate person' has the same meaning as in Section 9;

'the court' means a county court;

'prescribed' means prescribed by virtue of Section 27.

Excluded assignments

11.—(1) This section provides for the operation of Sections 5 to 10 in relation to assignments in breach of a covenant of a tenancy or assignments by operation of law ('excluded assignments').

(2) In the case of an excluded assignment Subsection (2) or (3) of Section 5—

Assignments in breach of covenant or by operation of law.

(a) shall not have the effect mentioned in that subsection in relation to the tenant as from that assignment, but

(b) shall have that effect as from the next assignment (if any) of the premises assigned by him which is not an excluded assignment.

(3) In the case of an excluded assignment Subsection (2) or (3) of Section 6 or 7—

    (a) shall not enable the landlord or former landlord to apply for such a release as is mentioned in that subsection as from that assignment, but

    (b) shall apply on the next assignment (if any) of the reversion assigned by the landlord which is not an excluded assignment so as to enable the landlord or former landlord to apply for any such release as from that subsequent assignment.

(4) Where Subsection (2) or (3) of Section 6 or 7 does so apply—

    (a) any reference in that section to the assignment (except where it relates to the time as from which the release takes effect) is a reference to the excluded assignment; but

    (b) in that excepted case and in Section 8 as it applies in relation to any application under that section made by virtue of Subsection (3) above, any reference to the assignment or proposed assignment is a reference to any such subsequent assignment as is mentioned in that subsection.

(5) In the case of an excluded assignment Section 9—

    (a) shall not enable the tenant or landlord and his assignee to apply for an agreed apportionment to become binding in accordance with Section 10 as from that assignment, but

    (b) shall apply on the next assignment (if any) of the premises or reversion assigned by the tenant or landlord which is not an excluded assignment so as to enable him and his assignee to apply for such an apportionment to become binding in accordance with Section 10 as from that subsequent assignment.

(6) Where Section 9 does so apply—

    (a) any reference in that section to the assignment or the assignee under it is a reference to the excluded assignment and the assignee under that assignment; but

    (b) in Section 10 as it applies in relation to any application under Section 9 made by virtue of Subsection (5) above, any reference to the assignment or proposed assignment is a reference to any such subsequent assignment as is mentioned in that subsection.

(7) If any such subsequent assignment as is mentioned in Subsection (2), (3) or (5) above comprises only part of the premises assigned by the tenant or (as the case may be) only part of the premises the reversion in which was assigned by the landlord on the excluded assignment—

    (a) the relevant provision or provisions of Section 5, 6, 7 or 9 shall only have the effect mentioned in that subsection to the extent that the covenants or covenant in question fall or falls to be complied with in relation to that part of those premises; and

    (b) that subsection may accordingly apply on different occasions in relation to different parts of those premises.

Third-party covenants

12.—(1) This section applies where—

(a) a person other than the landlord or tenant ('the third party') is under a covenant of a tenancy able (as principal) to discharge any function with respect to all or any of the demised premises ('the relevant function'); and

(b) that liability is not the liability of a guarantor or any other financial liability referable to the performance or otherwise of a covenant of the tenancy by another party to it.

Covenants with management companies etc.

(2) To the extent that any covenant of the tenancy confers any rights against the third party with respect to the relevant function, then for the purposes of the transmission of the benefit of the covenant in accordance with this Act it shall be treated as if it were—

(a) a tenant covenant of the tenancy to the extent that those rights are exercisable by the landlord; and

(b) a landlord covenant of the tenancy to the extent that those rights are exercisable by the tenant.

(3) To the extent that any covenant of the tenancy confers any rights exercisable by the third party with respect to the relevant function, then for the purposes mentioned in Subsection (4), it shall be treated as if it were—

(a) a tenant covenant of the tenancy to the extent that those rights are exercisable against the tenant; and

(b) a landlord covenant of the tenancy to the extent that those rights are exercisable against the landlord.

(4) The purposes mentioned in Subsection (3) are—

(a) the transmission of the burden of the covenant in accordance with this Act; and

(b) any release from, or apportionment of liability in respect of, the covenant in accordance with this Act.

(5) In relation to the release of the landlord from any covenant which is to be treated as a landlord covenant by virtue of Subsection (3), Section 8 shall apply as if any reference to the tenant were a reference to the third party.

Joint liability under covenants

13.—(1) Where in consequence of this Act two or more persons are bound by the same covenant, they are so bound both jointly and severally.

(2) Subject to Section 24(2), where by virtue of this Act—

(a) two or more persons are bound jointly and severally by the same covenant, and

(b) any of the persons so bound is released from the covenant, the release does not extend to any other of those persons.

Covenants binding two or more persons.

(3) For the purpose of providing for contribution between persons who,

by virtue of this Act, are bound jointly and severally by a covenant, the Civil Liability (Contribution) Act 1978 shall have effect as if—

(a) liability to a person under a covenant were liability in respect of damage suffered by that person;

(b) references to damage accordingly included a breach of a covenant of a tenancy; and

1978 c. 47.

(c) Section 7(2) of that Act were omitted.

14. The following provisions (by virtue of which indemnity covenants are implied on the assignment of a tenancy) shall cease to have effect—

(a) Subsections (1)(c) and (d) of Section 77 of the Law of Property Act 1925; and

Abolition of indemnity covenants implied by statute.

(b) Subsections (1)(b) and (2) of Section 24 of the Land Registration Act 1925.

Enforcement of covenants

1925 c. 20.
1925 c. 21.

15.—(1) Where any tenant covenant of a tenancy, or any right of re-entry contained in a tenancy, is enforceable by the reversioner in respect of any premises demised by the tenancy, it shall also be so enforceable by—

(a) any person (other than the reversioner) who, as the holder of the immediate reversion in those premises, is for the time being entitled to the rents and profits under the tenancy in respect of those premises, or

Enforcement of covenants.

(b) any mortgagee in possession of the reversion in those premises who is so entitled.

(2) Where any landlord covenant of a tenancy is enforceable against the reversioner in respect of any premises demised by the tenancy, it shall also be so enforceable against any person falling within Subsection (1)(a) or (b)

(3) Where any landlord covenant of a tenancy is enforceable by the tenant in respect of any premises demised by the tenancy, it shall also be so enforceable by any mortgagee in possession of those premises under a mortgage granted by the tenant.

(4) Where any tenant covenant of a tenancy, or any right of re-entry contained in a tenancy, is enforceable against the tenant in respect of any premises demised by the tenancy, it shall also be so enforceable against any such mortgagee.

(5) Nothing in this section shall operate—

(a) in the case of a covenant which (in whatever terms) is expressed to be personal to any person, to make the covenant enforceable by or (as the case may be) against any other person; or

(b) to make a covenant enforceable against any person if, apart from this section, it would not be enforceable against him by reason of its not having been registered under the Land Registration Act 1925 or the Land Charges Act 1972.

(6) In this section—

'mortgagee' and 'mortgage' include 'chargee' and 'charge' respectively;

'the reversioner', in relation to a tenancy, means the holder for the time being of the interest of the landlord under the tenancy.

1925 c. 21.
1972 c. 61.

Liability of former tenant etc in respect of covenants

16.—(1) Where on an assignment a tenant is to any extent released from a tenant covenant of a tenancy by virtue of this Act ('the relevant covenant'), nothing in this Act (and in particular Section 25) shall preclude him from entering into an authorised guarantee agreement with respect to the performance of that covenant by the assignee.

(2) For the purposes of this section an agreement is an authorised guarantee agreement if—

Tenant guaranteeing performance of covenant by assignee.

(a) under it the tenant guarantees the performance of the relevant covenant to any extent by the assignee; and

(b) it is entered into in the circumstances set out in Subsection (3); and

(c) its provisions conform with Subsections (4) and (5).

(3) Those circumstances are as follows—

(a) by virtue of a covenant against assignment (whether absolute or qualified) the assignment cannot be effected without the consent of the landlord under the tenancy or some other person;

(b) any such consent is given subject to a condition (lawfully imposed) that the tenant is to enter into an agreement guaranteeing the performance of the covenant by the assignee; and

(c) the agreement is entered into by the tenant in pursuance of that condition.

(4) An agreement is not an authorised guarantee agreement to the extent that it purports—

(a) to impose on the tenant any requirement to guarantee in any way the performance of the relevant covenant by any person other than the assignee; or

(b) to impose on the tenant any liability, restriction or other requirement (of whatever nature) in relation to any time after the assignee is released from that covenant by virtue of this Act.

(5) Subject to Subsection (4), an authorised guarantee agreement may—

(a) impose on the tenant any liability as sole or principal debtor in respect of any obligation owed by the assignee under the relevant covenant;

(b) impose on the tenant liabilities as guarantor in respect of the assignee's performance of that covenant which are no more onerous than those to which he would be subject in the event of his being liable as sole or principal debtor in respect of any obligation owed by the assignee under that covenant;

(c) require the tenant, in the event of the tenancy assigned by him being disclaimed, to enter into a new tenancy of the premises comprised in the assignment—

(i) whose term expires not later than the term of the tenancy assigned by the tenant, and

(ii) whose tenant covenants are no more onerous than those of that tenancy;

(d) make provision incidental or supplementary to any provision made by virtue of any of paragraphs (a) to (c).

(6) Where a person ('the former tenant') is to any extent released from a covenant of a tenancy by virtue of Section 11(2) as from an assignment and the assignor under the assignment enters into an authorised guarantee agreement with the landlord with respect to the performance of that covenant by the assignee under the assignment—

(a) the landlord may require the former tenant to enter into an agreement under which he guarantees, on terms corresponding to those of that authorised guarantee agreement, the performance of that covenant by the assignee under the assignment; and

(b) if its provisions conform with Subsections (4) and (5), any such agreement shall be an authorised guarantee agreement for the purposes of this section; and

(c) in the application of this section in relation to any such agreement—

(i) Subsections (2)(b) and (c) and (3) shall be omitted, and

(ii) any reference to the tenant or to the assignee shall be read as a reference to the former tenant or to the assignee under the assignment.

(7) For the purposes of Subsection (1) it is immaterial that—

(a) the tenant has already made an authorised guarantee agreement in respect of a previous assignment by him of the tenancy referred to in that subsection, it having been subsequently revested in him following a disclaimer on behalf of the previous assignee, or

(b) the tenancy referred to in that subsection is a new tenancy entered into by the tenant in pursuance of an authorised guarantee agreement;

and in any such case Subsections (2) to (5) shall apply accordingly.

(8) It is hereby declared that the rules of law relating to guarantees (and in particular those relating to the release of sureties) are, subject to its terms, applicable in relation to any authorised guarantee agreement as in relation to any other guarantee agreement.

17.—(1) This section applies where a person ('the former tenant') is as a result of an assignment no longer a tenant under a tenancy but—

(a) (in the case of a tenancy which is a new tenancy) he has under an authorised guarantee agreement guaranteed the performance by his assignee of a tenant covenant of the tenancy under which any fixed charge is payable; or

(b) (in the case of any tenancy) he remains bound by such a covenant.

Restriction on liability of former tenant or his guarantor for rent or service charge etc.

(2) The former tenant shall not be liable under that agreement or (as the case may be) the covenant to pay any amount in respect of any fixed charge payable under the covenant unless, within the period of six months beginning with the date when the charge becomes due, the landlord serves on the former tenant a notice informing him—

(a) that the charge is now due; and

(b) that in respect of the charge the landlord intends to recover from the former tenant such amount as is specified in the notice and (where payable) interest calculated on such basis as is so specified.

(3) Where a person ('the guarantor') has agreed to guarantee the performance by the former tenant of such a covenant as is mentioned in Subsection (1), the guarantor shall not be liable under the agreement to pay any amount in respect of any fixed charge payable under the covenant unless, within the period of six months beginning with the date when the charge becomes due, the landlord serves on the guarantor a notice informing him—

(a) that the charge is now due; and

(b) that in respect of the charge the landlord intends to recover from the guarantor such amount as is specified in the notice and (where payable) interest calculated on such basis as is so specified.

(4) Where the landlord has duly served a notice under Subsection (2) or (3), the amount (exclusive of interest) which the former tenant or (as the case may be) the guarantor is liable to pay in respect of the fixed charge in question shall not exceed the amount specified in the notice unless—

(a) his liability in respect of the charge is subsequently determined to be for a greater amount,

(b) the notice informed him of the possibility that that liability would be so determined, and

(c) within the period of three months beginning with the date of the determination, the landlord serves on him a further notice informing him that the landlord intends to recover that greater amount from him (plus interest, where payable).

(5) For the purposes of Subsection (2) or (3) any fixed charge which has become due before the date on which this Act comes into force shall

be treated as becoming due on that date; but neither of those subsections applies to any such charge if before that date proceedings have been instituted by the landlord for the recovery from the former tenant of any amount in respect of it.

(6) In this section—

'fixed charge', in relation to a tenancy, means—

(a) rent,

(b) any service charge as defined by Section 18 of the Landlord and Tenant Act 1985 (the words 'of a dwelling' being disregarded for this purpose), and

(c) any amount payable under a tenant covenant of the tenancy providing for the payment of a liquidated sum in the event of a failure to comply with any such covenant;

'landlord', in relation to a fixed charge, includes any person who has a right to enforce payment of the charge.

1985 c. 70.

18.—(1) This section applies where a person ('the former tenant') is as a result of an assignment no longer a tenant under a tenancy but—

(a) (in the case of a new tenancy) he has under an authorised guarantee agreement guaranteed the performance by his assignee of any tenant covenant of the tenancy; or

(b) (in the case of any tenancy) he remains bound by such a covenant.

(2) The former tenant shall not be liable under the agreement or (as the case may be) the covenant to pay any amount in respect of the covenant to the extent that the amount is referable to any relevant variation of the tenant covenants of the tenancy effected after the assignment.

(3) Where a person ('the guarantor') has agreed to guarantee the performance by the former tenant of a tenant covenant of the tenancy, the guarantor (where his liability to do so is not wholly discharged by any such variation of the tenant covenants of the tenancy) shall not be liable under the agreement to pay any amount in respect of the covenant to the extent that the amount is referable to any such variation.

(4) For the purposes of this section a variation of the tenant covenants of a tenancy is a 'relevant variation' if either—

(a) the landlord has, at the time of the variation, an absolute right to refuse to allow it; or

(b) the landlord would have had such a right if the variation had been sought by the former tenant immediately before the assignment by him but, between the time of that assignment and the time of the variation, the tenant covenants of the tenancy have been so varied as to deprive the landlord of such a right.

(5) In determining whether the landlord has or would have had such a right at any particular time regard shall be had to all the circumstances (including the effect of any provision made by or under any enactment).

Restriction of liability of former tenant or his guarantor where tenancy subsequently varied.

(6) Nothing in this section applies to any variation of the tenant covenants of a tenancy effected before the date on which this Act comes into force.

(7) In this section 'variation' means a variation whether effected by deed or otherwise.

Overriding leases

19.—(1) Where in respect of any tenancy ('the relevant tenancy') any person ('the claimant') makes full payment of an amount which he has been duly required to pay in accordance with Section 17, together with any interest payable, he shall be entitled (subject to and in accordance with this section) to have the landlord under that tenancy grant him an overriding lease of the premises demised by the tenancy.

(2) For the purposes of this section 'overriding lease' means a tenancy of the reversion expectant on the relevant tenancy which—

Right of former tenant or his guarantor to overriding lease.

(a) is granted for a term equal to the remainder of the term of the relevant tenancy plus three days or the longest period (less than three days) that will not wholly displace the landlord's reversionary interest expectant on the relevant tenancy, as the case may require; and

(b) (subject to Subsections (3) and (4) and to any modifications agreed to by the claimant and the landlord) otherwise contains the same covenants as the relevant tenancy, as they have effect immediately before the grant of the lease.

(3) An overriding lease shall not be required to reproduce any covenant of the relevant tenancy to the extent that the covenant is (in whatever terms) expressed to be a personal covenant between the landlord and the tenant under that tenancy.

(4) If any right, liability or other matter arising under a covenant of the relevant tenancy falls to be determined or otherwise operates (whether expressly or otherwise) by reference to the commencement of that tenancy—

(a) the corresponding covenant of the overriding lease shall be so framed that that right, liability or matter falls to be determined or otherwise operates by reference to the commencement of that tenancy; but

(b) the overriding lease shall not be required to reproduce any covenant of that tenancy to the extent that it has become spent by the time that that lease is granted.

(5) A claim to exercise the right to an overriding lease under this section is made by the claimant making a request for such a lease to the landlord; and any such request—

(a) must be made to the landlord in writing and specify the payment by virtue of which the claimant claims to be entitled to the lease ('the qualifying payment'); and

(b) must be so made at the time of making the qualifying payment or within the period of 12 months beginning with the date of that payment.

(6) Where the claimant duly makes such a request—

(a) the landlord shall (subject to Subsection (7)) grant and deliver to the claimant an overriding lease of the demised premises within a reasonable time of the request being received by the landlord; and

(b) the claimant—

(i) shall thereupon deliver to the landlord a counterpart of the lease duly executed by the claimant, and

(ii) shall be liable for the landlord's reasonable costs of and incidental to the grant of the lease.

(7) The landlord shall not be under any obligation to grant an overriding lease of the demised premises under this section at a time when the relevant tenancy has been determined; and a claimant shall not be entitled to the grant of such a lease if at the time when he makes his request—

(a) the landlord has already granted such a lease and that lease remains in force; or

(b) another person has already duly made a request for such a lease to the landlord and that request has been neither withdrawn nor abandoned by that person.

(8) Where two or more requests are duly made on the same day, then for the purposes of Subsection (7)—

(a) a request made by a person who was liable for the qualifying payment as a former tenant shall be treated as made before a request made by a person who was so liable as a guarantor; and

(b) a request made by a person whose liability in respect of the covenant in question commenced earlier than any such liability of another person shall be treated as made before a request made by that other person.

(9) Where a claimant who has duly made a request for an overriding lease under this section subsequently withdraws or abandons the request before he is granted such a lease by the landlord, the claimant shall be liable for the landlord's reasonable costs incurred in pursuance of the request down to the time of its withdrawal or abandonment; and for the purposes of this section—

(a) a claimant's request is withdrawn by the claimant notifying the landlord in writing that he is withdrawing his request; and

(b) a claimant is to be regarded as having abandoned his request if—

(i) the landlord has requested the claimant in writing to take, within such reasonable period as is specified in the landlord's request, all or any of the remaining steps required to be taken by the claimant before the lease can be granted, and

(ii) the claimant fails to comply with the landlord's request,

and is accordingly to be regarded as having abandoned it at the time when that period expires.

(10) Any request or notification under this section may be sent by post.

(11) The preceding provisions of this section shall apply where the landlord is the tenant under an overriding lease granted under this section as they apply where no such lease has been granted; and accordingly there may be two or more such leases interposed between the first such lease and the relevant tenancy.

20.—(1) For the purposes of Section 1 an overriding lease shall be a new tenancy only if the relevant tenancy is a new tenancy.

(2) Every overriding lease shall state—

(a) that it is a lease granted under Section 19, and

(b) whether it is or is not a new tenancy for the purposes of Section 1;

and any such statement shall comply with such requirements as may be prescribed by rules made in pursuance of Section 144 of the Land Registration Act 1925 (power to make general rules).

Overriding leases: supplementary provisions.

(3) A claim that the landlord has failed to comply with Subsection (6)(a) of Section 19 may be made the subject of civil proceedings in like manner as any other claim in tort for breach of statutory duty; and if the claimant under that section fails to comply with Subsection (6)(b)(i) of that section he shall not be entitled to exercise any of the rights otherwise exercisable by him under the overriding lease.

1925 c. 21.

(4) An overriding lease—

(a) shall be deemed to be authorised as against the persons interested in any mortgage of the landlord's interest (however created or arising); and

(b) shall be binding on any such persons;

and if any such person is by virtue of such a mortgage entitled to possession of the documents of title relating to the landlord's interest—

(i) the landlord shall within one month of the execution of the lease deliver to that person the counterpart executed in pursuance of Section 19(6)(b)(i); and

(ii) if he fails to do so, the instrument creating or evidencing the mortgage shall apply as if the obligation to deliver a counterpart were included in the terms of the mortgage as set out in that instrument.

(5) It is hereby declared—

(a) that the fact that an overriding lease takes effect subject to the relevant tenancy shall not constitute a breach of any covenant of the lease against subletting or parting with possession of the premises demised by the lease or any part of them; and

(b) that each of Sections 16, 17 and 18 applies where the tenancy referred to in Subsection (1) of that section is an overriding lease as it applies in other cases falling within that subsection.

(6) No tenancy shall be registrable under the Land Charges Act 1972 or be taken to be an estate contract within the meaning of that Act by reason of any right or obligation that may arise under Section 19, and any right arising from a request made under that section shall not be an overriding interest within the meaning of the Land Registration Act 1925; but any such request shall be registrable under the Land Charges Act 1972, or may be the subject of a notice or caution under the Land Registration Act 1925, as if it were an estate contract.

1972 c. 61.

(7) In this section—

(a) 'mortgage' includes 'charge'; and

1972 c. 61.
1925 c. 21.

(b) any expression which is also used in Section 19 has the same meaning as in that section.

Forfeiture and disclaimer

21.—(1) Where—

(a) as a result of one or more assignments a person is the tenant of part only of the premises demised by a tenancy, and

(b) under a proviso or stipulation in the tenancy there is a right of re-entry or forfeiture for a breach of a tenant covenant of the tenancy, and

(c) the right is (apart from this subsection) exercisable in relation to that part and other land demised by the tenancy,

the right shall nevertheless, in connection with a breach of any such covenant by that person, be taken to be a right exercisable only in relation to that part.

Forfeiture or
disclaimer
limited to part
only of demised
premises.

(2) Where—

(a) a company which is being wound up, or a trustee in bankruptcy, is as a result of one or more assignments the tenant of part only of the premises demised by a tenancy, and

(b) the liquidator of the company exercises his power under Section 178 of the Insolvency Act 1986, or the trustee in bankruptcy exercises his power under Section 315 of that Act, to disclaim property demised by the tenancy,

the power is exercisable only in relation to the part of the premises referred to in paragraph (a).

1986 c. 45.

Landlord's consent to assignments

22. After Subsection (1) of Section 19 of the Landlord and Tenant Act 1927 (provisions as to covenants not to assign etc without licence or consent) there shall be inserted—

'(1A) Where the landlord and the tenant under a qualifying lease have entered into an agreement specifying for the purposes of this subsection—

Imposition of conditions regulating giving of landlord's consent to assignments. 1927 c. 36.

(a) any circumstances in which the landlord may withhold his licence or consent to an assignment of the demised premises or any part of them, or

(b) any conditions subject to which any such licence or consent may be granted,

then the landlord—

(i) shall not be regarded as unreasonably withholding his licence or consent to any such assignment if he withholds it on the ground (and it is the case) that any such circumstances exist, and

(ii) if he gives any such licence or consent subject to any such conditions, shall not be regarded as giving it subject to unreasonable conditions;

and Section 1 of the Landlord and Tenant Act 1988 (qualified duty to consent to assignment etc) shall have effect subject to the provisions of this subsection.

(1B) Subsection (1A) of this section applies to such an agreement as is mentioned in that subsection—

(a) whether it is contained in the lease or not, and

(b) whether it is made at the time when the lease is granted or at any other time falling before the application for the landlord's licence or consent is made.

(1C) Subsection (1A) shall not, however, apply to any such agreement to the extent that any circumstances or conditions specified in it are framed by reference to any matter falling to be determined by the landlord or by any other person for the purposes of the agreement, unless under the terms of the agreement—

(a) that person's power to determine that matter is required to be exercised reasonably, or

(b) the tenant is given an unrestricted right to have any such determination reviewed by a person independent of both landlord and tenant whose identity is ascertainable by reference to the agreement,

and in the latter case the agreement provides for the determination made by any such independent person on the review to be conclusive as to the matter in question.

(1D) In its application to a qualifying lease, Subsection (l)(b) of this section shall not have effect in relation to any assignment of the lease.

(1E) In Subsections (1A) and (1D) of this section—

(a) 'qualifying lease' means any lease which is a new tenancy for the purposes of Section 1 of the Landlord and Tenant

(Covenants) Act 1995 other than a residential lease, namely
a lease by which a building or part of a building is let wholly
or mainly as a single private residence; and

(b) references to assignment include parting with possession
on assignment.'

Supplemental

3.—(1) Where as a result of an assignment a person becomes, by virtue
of this Act, bound by or entitled to the benefit of a covenant, he shall not
by virtue of this Act have any liability or rights under the covenant in
relation to any time falling before the assignment.

(2) Subsection (1) does not preclude any such rights being expressly
assigned to the person in question.

Effects of becoming subject to liability under, or entitled to benefit of, covenant etc.

(3) Where as a result of an assignment a person becomes, by virtue of
this Act, entitled to a right of re-entry contained in a tenancy, that right shall
be exercisable in relation to any breach of a covenant of the tenancy
occurring before the assignment as in relation to one occurring thereafter
unless by reason of any waiver or release it was not so exercisable
immediately before the assignment.

24.—(1) Any release of a person from a covenant by virtue of this Act
does not affect any liability of his arising from a breach of the covenant
occurring before the release.

(2) Where—

(a) by virtue of this Act a tenant is released from a tenant covenant
of a tenancy, and

Effects of release from liability under, or loss of benefit of, covenant.

(b) immediately before the release another person is bound by a
covenant of the tenancy imposing any liability or penalty in the
event of a failure to comply with that tenant covenant,

then, as from the release of the tenant, that other person is released from
the covenant mentioned in paragraph (b) to the same extent as the tenant
is released from that tenant covenant.

(3) Where a person bound by a landlord or tenant covenant of a
tenancy—

(a) assigns the whole or part of his interest in the premises demised
by the tenancy, but

(b) is not released by virtue of this Act from the covenant (with the
result that Subsection (1) does not apply),

the assignment does not affect any liability of his arising from a breach
of the covenant occurring before the assignment.

(4) Where by virtue of this Act a person ceases to be entitled to the
benefit of a covenant, this does not affect any rights of his arising from a
breach of the covenant occurring before he ceases to be so entitled.

25.—(1) Any agreement relating to a tenancy is void to the extent that—

(a) it would apart from this section have effect to exclude, modify or otherwise frustrate the operation of any provision of this Act, or

(b) it provides for—

(i) the termination or surrender of the tenancy, or

(ii) the imposition on the tenant of any penalty, disability or liability, in the event of the operation of any provision of this Act, or

(c) it provides for any of the matters referred to in paragraph (b)(i) or (ii) and does so (whether expressly or otherwise) in connection with, or in consequence of, the operation of any provision of this Act.

Agreement void if it restricts operation of the Act.

(2) To the extent that an agreement relating to a tenancy constitutes a covenant (whether absolute or qualified) against the assignment, or parting with the possession, of the premises demised by the tenancy or any part of them—

(a) the agreement is not void by virtue of Subsection (1) by reason only of the fact that as such the covenant prohibits or restricts any such assignment or parting with possession; but

(b) paragraph (a) above does not otherwise affect the operation of that subsection in relation to the agreement (and in particular does not preclude its application to the agreement to the extent that it purports to regulate the giving of, or the making of any application for, consent to any such assignment or parting with possession).

(3) In accordance with Section 16(1) nothing in this section applies to any agreement to the extent that it is an authorised guarantee agreement but (without prejudice to the generality of Subsection (1) above) an agreement is void to the extent that it is one falling within Section 16(4)(a) or (b).

(4) This section applies to an agreement relating to a tenancy whether or not the agreement is—

(a) contained in the instrument creating the tenancy; or

(b) made before the creation of the tenancy.

26.—(1) Nothing in this Act is to be read as preventing—

(a) a party to a tenancy from releasing a person from a landlord covenant or a tenant covenant of the tenancy; or

(b) the parties to a tenancy from agreeing to an apportionment of liability under such a covenant.

Miscellaneous savings etc.

(2) Nothing in this Act affects the operation of Section 3(3A) of the Landlord and Tenant Act 1985 (preservation of former landlord's liability until tenant notified of new landlord).

1985 c. 70.

(3) No apportionment which has become binding in accordance with Section 10 shall be affected by any order or decision made under or by virtue of any enactment not contained in this Act which relates to apportionment.

27.—(1) The form of any notice to be served for the purposes of Section 8, 10 or 17 shall be prescribed by regulations made by the Lord Chancellor by statutory instrument.

(2) The regulations shall require any notice served for the purposes of Section 8(1) or 10(1) ('the initial notice') to include—

Notices for the purposes of the Act.

(a) an explanation of the significance of the notice and the options available to the person on whom it is served;

(b) a statement that any objections to the proposed release, or (as the case may be) to the proposed binding effect of the apportionment, must be made by notice in writing served on the person or persons by whom the initial notice is served within the period of four weeks beginning with the day on which the initial notice is served; and

(c) an address in England and Wales to which any such objections may be sent.

(3) The regulations shall require any notice served for the purposes of Section 17 to include an explanation of the significance of the notice.

(4) If any notice purporting to be served for the purposes of Section 8(1), 10(1) or 17 is not in the prescribed form, or in a form substantially to the same effect, the notice shall not be effective for the purposes of Section 8, Section 10 or Section 17 (as the case may be).

(5) Section 23 of the Landlord and Tenant Act 1927 shall apply in relation to the service of notices for the purposes of Section 8, 10 or 17.

(6) Any statutory instrument made under this section shall be subject to annulment in pursuance of a resolution of either House of Parliament.

1927 c. 36

28.—(1) In this Act (unless the context otherwise requires)—

'assignment' includes equitable assignment and in addition (subject to Section 11) assignment in breach of a covenant of a tenancy or by operation of law;

Interpretation.

'authorised guarantee agreement' means an agreement which is an authorised guarantee agreement for the purposes of Section 16;

'collateral agreement', in relation to a tenancy, means any agreement collateral to the tenancy, whether made before or after its creation;

'consent' includes licence;

'covenant' includes term, condition and obligation, and references to a covenant (or any description of covenant) of a tenancy include a covenant (or a covenant of that description) contained in a collateral agreement;

'landlord' and 'tenant', in relation to a tenancy, mean the person for the time being entitled to the reversion expectant on the term of the tenancy and the person so entitled to that term respectively;

'landlord covenant', in relation to a tenancy, means a covenant falling to be complied with by the landlord of premises demised by the tenancy;

'new tenancy' means a tenancy which is a new tenancy for the purposes of Section 1;

'reversion' means the interest expectant on the termination of a tenancy;

'tenancy' means any lease or other tenancy and includes—

(a) a subtenancy, and

(b) an agreement for a tenancy,

but does not include a mortgage term;

'tenant covenant', in relation to a tenancy, means a covenant falling to be complied with by the tenant of premises demised by the tenancy.

(2) For the purposes of any reference in this Act to a covenant falling to be complied with in relation to a particular part of the premises demised by a tenancy, a covenant falls to be so complied with if—

(a) it in terms applies to that part of the premises, or

(b) in its practical application it can be attributed to that part of the premises (whether or not it can also be so attributed to other individual parts of those premises).

(3) Subsection (2) does not apply in relation to covenants to pay money; and, for the purposes of any reference in this Act to a covenant falling to be complied with in relation to a particular part of the premises demised by a tenancy, a covenant of a tenancy which is a covenant to pay money falls to be so complied with if—

(a) the covenant in terms applies to that part; or

(b) the amount of the payment is determinable specifically by reference—

(i) to that part, or

(ii) to anything falling to be done by or for a person as tenant or occupier of that part (if it is a tenant covenant), or

(iii) to anything falling to be done by or for a person as landlord of that part (if it is a landlord covenant).

(4) Where two or more persons jointly constitute either the landlord or the tenant in relation to a tenancy, any reference in this Act to the landlord or the tenant is a reference to both or all of the persons who jointly constitute the landlord or the tenant, as the case may be (and accordingly nothing in Section 13 applies in relation to the rights and liabilities of such persons between themselves).

(5) References in this Act to the assignment by a landlord of the

reversion in the whole or part of the premises demised by a tenancy are to the assignment by him of the whole of his interest (as owner of the reversion) in the whole or part of those premises.

(6) For the purposes of this Act—

(a) any assignment (however effected) consisting in the transfer of the whole of the landlord's interest (as owner of the reversion) in any premises demised by a tenancy shall be treated as an assignment by the landlord of the reversion in those premises even if it is not effected by him; and

(b) any assignment (however effected) consisting in the transfer of the whole of the tenant's interest in any premises demised by a tenancy shall be treated as an assignment by the tenant of those premises even if it is not effected by him.

29. This Act binds the Crown.

30.—(1) The enactments specified in Schedule 1 are amended in accordance with that Schedule, the amendments being consequential on the provisions of this Act.

(2) The enactments specified in Schedule 2 are repealed to the extent specified.

Crown
application.

Consequential
amendments
and repeals.

(3) Subsections (1) and (2) do not affect the operation of—

(a) Section 77 of, or Part IX or X of Schedule 2 to, the Law of Property Act 1925, or

(b) Section 24(1)(b) or (2) of the Land Registration Act 1925,

in relation to tenancies which are not new tenancies.

(4) In consequence of this Act nothing in the following provisions, namely—

1925 c. 20.

(a) Sections 78 and 79 of the Law of Property Act 1925 (benefit and burden of covenants relating to land), and

1925 c. 21.

(b) Sections 141 and 142 of that Act (running of benefit and burden of covenants with reversion),

shall apply in relation to new tenancies.

(5) The Lord Chancellor may by order made by statutory instrument make, in the case of such enactments as may be specified in the order, such amendments or repeals in, or such modifications of, those enactments as appear to him to be necessary or expedient in consequence of any provision of this Act.

(6) Any statutory instrument made under Subsection (5) shall be subject to annulment in pursuance of a resolution of either House of Parliament.

31.—(1) The provisions of this Act come into force on such day as the Lord Chancellor may appoint by order made by statutory instrument.

(2) An order under this section may contain such transitional provisions

and savings (whether or not involving the modification of any enactment) as appear to the Lord Chancellor necessary or expedient in connection with the provisions brought into force by the order.

Commencement

32.—(1) This Act may be cited as the Landlord and Tenant (Covenants) Act 1995.

(2) This Act extends to England and Wales only.

Short title and extent.

SCHEDULES

Section 30(1)

SCHEDULE I

CONSEQUENTIAL AMENDMENTS

Trustee Act 1925 (c.19)

1. In Section 26 of the Trustee Act 1925 (protection against liability in respect of rents and covenants), after Subsection (1) insert—

'(1A) Where a personal representative or trustee has as such entered into, or may as such be required to enter into, an authorised guarantee agreement with respect to any lease comprised in the estate of a deceased testator or intestate or a trust estate (and, in a case where he has entered into such an agreement, he has satisfied all liabilities under it which may have accrued and been claimed up to the date of distribution—

(a) he may distribute the residuary real and personal estate of the deceased testator or intestate, or the trust estate, to or amongst the persons entitled thereto—

(i) without appropriating any part of the estate of the deceased, or the trust estate, to meet any future liability (or, as the case may be, any liability) under any such agreement, and

(ii) notwithstanding any potential liability of his to enter into any such agreement; and

(b) notwithstanding such distribution, he shall not be personally liable in respect of any subsequent claim (or, as the case may be, any claim) under any such agreement.

In this subsection 'authorised guarantee agreement' has the same meaning as in the Landlord and Tenant (Covenants) Act 1995.'

Law of Property Act 1925 (c.20)

2. In Section 77 of the Law of Property Act 1925 (implied covenants in conveyances subject to rents), for Subsection (2) substitute—

'(2) Where in a conveyance for valuable consideration, other than a mortgage, part of land affected by a rentcharge is, without the consent of the owner of the rentcharge, expressed to be conveyed subject to or charged with the entire rent, paragraph (B)(i) of Subsection (1) of this section shall apply as if, in paragraph (i) of Part VIII of the Second Schedule to this Act—

(a) any reference to the apportioned rent were to the entire rent; and

(b) the words '(other than the covenant to pay the entire rent)' were omitted.

(2A) Where in a conveyance for valuable consideration, other than a mortgage, part of land affected by a rentcharge is, without the consent of the owner of the rentcharge, expressed to be conveyed discharged or exonerated from the entire rent, paragraph (B)(ii) of Subsection (1) of this section shall apply as if, in paragraph (ii) of Part VIII of the Second Schedule to this Act—

(a) any reference to the balance of the rent were to the entire rent; and

(b) the words, 'other than the covenant to pay the entire rent,' were omitted.'

Landlord and Tenant Act 1954 (c.56)

3. At the end of Section 34 of the Landlord and Tenant Act 1954 (rent under new tenancy) insert—

'(4) It is hereby declared that the matters which are to be taken into account by the court in determining the rent include any effect on rent of the operation of the provisions of the Landlord and Tenant (Covenants) Act 1995.'

4.—(1) The existing provisions of Section 35 of that Act (other terms of new tenancy) shall constitute Subsection (1) of that section.

(2) After those provisions insert—

'(2) In Subsection (1) of this section the reference to all relevant circumstances includes (without prejudice to the generality of that reference) a reference to the operation of the provisions of the Landlord and Tenant (Covenants) Act 1995.'

SCHEDULE 2

Section 30(2).

REPEALS

Chapter	Short title	Extent of repeal
15 and 16 Geo.5 c.20.	Law of Property Act 1925.	In Section 77, subsection (1)(c) and (d) and, in subsection (7), paragraph (c) and the 'or' preceding it. In Schedule 2, Parts IX and X.
15 and 16 Geo.5 c. 21.	Land Registration Act 1925.	Section 24(1)(b) and (2).

Appendix II

STATUTORY INSTRUMENTS

1995 No. 2964

LANDLORD AND TENANT, ENGLAND AND WALES

The Landlord and Tenant (Covenants) Act 1995 (Notices) Regulations 1995

Made	*9th November 1995*
Laid before Parliament	*20th November 1995*
Coming into force	*1st January 1996*

The Lord Chancellor, in exercise of the powers conferred on him by Section 27 of the Landlord and Tenant (Covenants) Act 1995(a), hereby makes the following Regulations:

1.—(1) These Regulations may be cited as the Landlord and Tenant (Covenants) Act 1995 (Notices) Regulations 1995 and shall come into force on 1 January 1996.

(2) In these Regulations, 'the Act' means the Landlord and Tenant (Covenants) Act 1995, and a form referred to by number means the form so numbered in the Schedule to these Regulations.

2. The forms prescribed for the purposes of the Act shall be as follows, or in each case a form substantially to the like effect:

PURPOSE OF NOTICE	FORM TO BE USED
(a) (i) Landlord informing a former tenant or guarantor of such a tenant of an amount payable in respect of a fixed charge under a covenant of the tenancy which the landlord intends to recover from that person under Section 17 of the Act	Form 1
(ii) Landlord informing a former tenant or guarantor of such a tenant of a revised, greater amount payable in respect of a fixed charge under a covenant of the tenancy which the landlord intends to recover from that person under Section 17 of the Act	Form 2
(b) (i) Landlord applying to be released from all the landlord covenants of the tenancy on assignment of his entire interest under Sections 6 and 8 of the Act	Whole of Form 3 (landlord to complete Part I only)
(ii) Tenant objecting to the landlord's release under Section 8 of the Act	Part II of Form 3
(iii) Tenant consenting to the landlord's release and withdrawing a notice objecting to such release under Section 8 of the Act	Notice in writing stating that tenant is now consenting and that the notice of objections is withdrawn
(c) (i) Landlord applying to be released from the landlord covenants of the tenancy to the appropriate extent on assignment of part only of his interest under Sections 6 and 8 of the Act	Whole of Form 4 (landlord to complete Part I only)
(ii) Tenant objecting to the landlord's release under Section 8 of the Act	Part II of Form 4
(iii) Tenant consenting to the landlord's release and withdrawing a notice objecting to such release under Section 8 of the Act	Notice in writing stating that tenant is now consenting and that the notice of objection is withdrawn

PURPOSE OF NOTICE	FORM TO BE USED
(d) (i) Former landlord applying to be released from all the landlord covenants of the tenancy on a subsequent assignment of the landlord's interest under Sections 7 and 8 of the Act	Whole of Form 5 (landlord to complete Part I only)
(ii) Tenant objecting to the former landlord's release under Section 8 of the Act	Part II of Form 5
(iii) Tenant consenting to the former landlord's release and withdrawing a notice objecting to such release under Section 8 of the Act	Notice in writing stating that tenant is now consenting and that the notice of objection is withdrawn
(e) (i) Former landlord who assigned part only of his interest applying to be released from the landlord covenants of the tenancy to the appropriate extent on a subsequent assignment of the landlord's interest under Sections 7 and 8 of the Act	Whole of Form 6 (landlord to complete Part I only)
(ii) Tenant objecting to the former landlord's release under Section 8 of the Act	Part II of Form 6
(iii) Tenant consenting to the former landlord's release and with drawing a notice objecting to such release under Section 8 of the Act	Notice in writing stating that tenant is now consenting and that the notice of objection is withdrawn
(f) (i) Tenant and tenant's assignee jointly applying for an apportionment of liability under the covenants of the tenancy to become to binding on the appropriate person under Sections 9 and 10 of the Act	Whole of Form 7 (tenant and assignee to complete Part I only)
(ii) Appropriate person objecting to the apportionment becoming binding on that person under Section 10 of the Act	Part II of Form 7
(iii) Appropriate person consenting to the apportionment becoming binding on that person and withdrawing a notice objecting to the apportionment becoming so binding under Section 10 of the Act	Notice in writing stating that appropriate person isn now consenting and that the notice of objection is

PURPOSE OF NOTICE	FORM TO BE USED
(g) (i) Landlord and landlord's assignee jointly applying for an apportionment of liability under the covenants of the tenancy to become binding on the appropriate person under Sections 9 and 10 of the Act	Whole of Form 8 (landlord and assignee to complete Part I only)
(ii) Appropriate person objecting to the apportionment becoming binding on that person under Section 10 of the Act	Part II of Form 8
(iii) Appropriate person consenting to the apportionment becoming binding on that person and withdrawing a notice objecting to the apportionment becoming so binding under Section 10 of the Act	Notice in writing stating that appropriate person is now consenting and that the notice of objection is withdrawn

Dated 9th November 1995   *Mackay of Clashfern*, C.

SCHEDULE

FORM 1

NOTICE TO FORMER TENANT OR GUARANTOR OF INTENTION TO RECOVER FIXED CHARGE[1]
(Landlord and Tenant (Covenants) Act 1995, Section 17)

To [name and address]: . . . .

. . . .

IMPORTANT – THE PERSON GIVING THIS NOTICE IS PROTECTING THE RIGHT TO RECOVER THE AMOUNT(S) SPECIFIED FROM YOU NOW OR AT SOME TIME IN THE FUTURE. THERE MAY BE ACTION WHICH YOU CAN TAKE TO PROTECT YOUR POSITION. READ THE NOTICE AND ALL THE NOTES OVERLEAF CAREFULLY. IF YOU ARE IN ANY DOUBT ABOUT THE ACTION YOU SHOULD TAKE, SEEK ADVICE IMMEDIATELY, FOR INSTANCE FROM A SOLICITOR OR CITIZENS' ADVICE BUREAU.

---

1. This notice is given under Section 17 of the Landlord and Tenant (Covenants) Act 1995. {see Note 1 overleaf}

2. It relates to (address and description of property) . . . .

. . . .

let under a lease dated . . . . and made between . . . .

. . . .

. . . .

[of which you were formerly tenant] [in relation to which you are liable as guarantor of a person who was formerly tenant].[2]

3. I/we as landlord[3] hereby give you notice that the fixed charge(s) of which details are set out in the attached Schedule[4] is/are now due and unpaid, and that I/we intend to recover from you the amount(s) specified in the Schedule [and interest from the date and calculated on the basis specified in the Schedule][5]. {see Notes 2 and 3 overleaf}

---

1   The Act defines a fixed charge as (a) rent, (b) any service charge (as defined by Section 18 of the Landlord and Tenant Act 1985, disregarding the words 'of a dwelling') and (c) any amount payable under a tenant covenant of the tenancy providing for payment of a liquidated sum in the event of failure to comply with the covenant.

2   Delete alternative as appropriate.

3   'Landlord' for these purposes includes any person who has the right to enforce the charge.

4   The Schedule must be in writing, and must indicate in relation to each item the date on which it became payable, the amount payable and whether it is rent, service charge or a fixed charge of some other kind (in which case particulars of the nature of the charge should be given). Charges due before 1 January 1996 are deemed to have become due on that date, but the actual date on which they became due should also be stated.

5   Delete words in brackets if not applicable. If applicable, the Schedule must state the basis on which interest is calculated (for example, rate of interest, date from which it is payable and provision of Lease or other document under which it is payable).

4.[1] There is a possibility that your liability in respect of the fixed charge(s) detailed in the Schedule will subsequently be determined to be for a greater amount. *[see Note 4 below]*

5. All correspondence about this notice should be sent to the landlord/landlord's agent at the address given below.

Date............ Signature of landlord/landlord's agent ....

Name and address of landlord..

....

....

[Name and address of agent ....

....

....]

NOTES

1. The person giving you this notice alleges that you are still liable for the performance of the tenant's obligations under the tenancy to which this notice relates, either as a previous tenant bound by privity of contract or an authorised guarantee agreement, or because you are the guarantor of a previous tenant. By giving you this notice, the landlord (or other person entitled to enforce payment, such as a management company) is protecting his right to require you to pay the amount specified in the notice. There may be other sums not covered by the notice which the landlord can also recover because they are not fixed charges (for example in respect of repairs or costs if legal proceedings have to be brought). If you pay the amount specified in this notice in full, you will have the right to call on the landlord to grant you an 'overriding lease', which puts you in the position of landlord to the present tenant. There are both advantages and drawbacks to doing this, and you should take advice before coming to a decision.

Validity of notice

2. The landlord is required to give this notice within six months of the date on which the charge or charges in question became due (or, if it became due before 1 January 1996, within six months of that date). If the notice has been given late, it is not valid and the amount in the notice cannot be recovered from you. The date of the giving of the notice may not be the date written on the notice or the date on which you actually saw it. It may, for instance, be the date on which the notice was delivered through the post to your last address known to the landlord. If you are in any doubt, you should seek advice immediately.

---

1 Delete this paragraph if not applicable. If applicable (for example, where there is an outstanding rent review or service charge collected on account) a further notice must be served on the former tenant or guarantor within three (3) months beginning with the date on which the greater amount is determined. If only applicable to one or more charge of several, the Schedule should specify which.

Interest

3. If interest is payable on the amount due, the landlord does not have to state the precise amount of interest, but he must state the basis on which the interest is calculated to enable you to work out the likely amount, or he will not be able to claim interest at all. This does not include interest which may be payable under rules of court if legal proceedings are brought.

Change in amount due

4. Apart from interest, the landlord is not entitled to recover an amount which is more than he has specified in the notice, with one exception. This is where the amount cannot be finally determined within six months after it is due (for example, if there is dispute concerning an outstanding rent review or if the charge is a service charge collected on account and adjusted following final determination). In such a case, if the amount due is eventually determined to be more than originally notified, the landlord may claim the larger amount *if and only if* he completes the paragraph giving notice of the possibility that the amount may change, and gives a further notice specifying the larger amount within three months of the final determination.

FORM 2

FURTHER NOTICE TO FORMER TENANT OR GUARANTOR OF REVISED AMOUNT DUE IN RESPECT OF A FIXED CHARGE[1]
(Landlord and Tenant (Covenants) Act 1995, Section 17)

To [name and address]: . . . .

. . . .

> IMPORTANT – THE PERSON GIVING THIS NOTICE IS PROTECTING THE RIGHT TO RECOVER THE AMOUNT(S) SPECIFIED FROM YOU NOW OR AT SOME TIME IN THE FUTURE. THERE MAY BE ACTION WHICH YOU CAN TAKE TO PROTECT YOUR POSITION. READ THE NOTICE AND ALL THE NOTES OVERLEAF CAREFULLY. IF YOU ARE IN ANY DOUBT ABOUT THE ACTION YOU SHOULD TAKE, SEEK ADVICE IMMEDIATELY, FOR INSTANCE FROM A SOLICITOR OR CITIZENS' ADVICE BUREAU.

1. This notice is given under Section 17 of the Landlord and Tenant (Covenants) Act 1995. *[see Note 1 overleaf]*

2. It relates to (address and description of property) . . . .

. . . .

let under a lease dated . . . . and made between . . . .

. . . .

. . . .

[of which you were formerly tenant] [in relation to which you are liable as guarantor of a person who was formerly tenant].[2]

3. You were informed on . . . . (date of original notice) of the amount due in respect of a fixed charge or charges, and of the possibility that your liability in respect of the charge(s) might subsequently be determined to be for a greater amount.

4. I/we as landlord[3] hereby give you notice that the fixed charge(s) of which details are set out in the attached Schedule[4] has/have now been determined to be for a greater amount than specified in the original notice, and that I/we intend to recover from you the amount(s) specified in the Schedule [and interest from the date and calculated on the basis specified in the Schedule][5]. *[see Notes 2 and 3 overleaf]*

---

1 The Act defines a fixed charge as (a) rent, (b) any service charge (as defined by Section 18 of the Landlord and Tenant Act 1985, disregarding the words 'of a dwelling') and (c) any amount payable under a tenant covenant of the tenancy providing for payment of a liquidated sum in the event of failure to comply with the covenant.

2 Delete alternative as appropriate.

3 'Landlord' for these purposes includes any person who has the right to enforce the charge.

4 The Schedule can be in any form, but must indicate in relation to each item the date on which it was revised, the revised amount payable and whether it is rent, service charge or a fixed charge of some other kind (in which case particulars of the nature of the charge should be given).

5 Delete words in brackets if not applicable. If applicable, the Schedule must state the basis on which interest is calculated (for example, rate of interest, date from which it is payable and provision of Lease or other document under which it is payable).

5. All correspondence about this notice should be sent to the landlord/landlord' s agent at the address given below.

Date.............Signature of landlord/landlord's agent ....

Name and address of landlord......................................

....

....

[Name and address of agent ....

....

....]

NOTES

1. The person giving you this notice alleges that you are still liable for the performance of the tenant's obligations under the tenancy to which this notice relates, either as a previous tenant bound by privity of contract or an authorised guarantee agreement, or because you are the guarantor of a previous tenant. You should already have been given a notice by which the landlord (or other person entitled to enforce payment, such as a management company) protected his right to require you to pay the amount specified in that notice. The purpose of this notice is to protect the landlord' s right to require you to pay a larger amount, because the amount specified in the original notice could not be finally determined at the time of the original notice (for example, because there was a dispute concerning an outstanding rent review or if the charge was a service charge collected on account and adjusted following final determination).

Validity of notice

2. The notice is not valid unless the original notice contained a warning that the amount in question might subsequently be determined to be greater. In addition, the landlord is required to give this notice within three months of the date on which the amount was finally determined. If the original notice did not include that warning, or if this notice has been given late, then this notice is not valid and the landlord cannot recover the greater amount, but only the smaller amount specified in the original notice. The date of the giving of this notice may not be the date written on the notice or the date on which you actually saw it. It may, for instance, be the date on which the notice was delivered through the post to your last address known to the person giving notice. If you are in any doubt, you should seek advice immediately.

Interest

3. If interest is chargeable on the amount due, the landlord does not have to state the precise amount of interest, but he must have stated the basis on which the interest is calculated, or he will not be able to claim interest at all.

FORM 3

PART I

LANDLORD'S NOTICE APPLYING FOR RELEASE FROM LANDLORD COVENANTS OF A TENANCY ON ASSIGNMENT OF WHOLE OF REVERSION
(Landlord and Tenant (Covenants) Act 1995, Sections 6 and 8)

To [name and address]: . . . .

. . . .

IMPORTANT – THE PERSON GIVING THIS NOTICE IS PROTECTING THE RIGHT TO RECOVER THE AMOUNT(S) SPECIFIED FROM YOU NOW OR AT SOME TIME IN THE FUTURE. THERE MAY BE ACTION WHICH YOU CAN TAKE TO PROTECT YOUR POSITION. READ THE NOTICE AND ALL THE NOTES OVERLEAF CAREFULLY. IF YOU ARE IN ANY DOUBT ABOUT THE ACTION YOU SHOULD TAKE, SEEK ADVICE IMMEDIATELY, FOR INSTANCE FROM A SOLICITOR OR CITIZENS' ADVICE BUREAU.

---

1. This notice is given under Section 17 of the Landlord and Tenant (Covenants) Act 1995. *[see Note 1 overleaf]*

2. It relates to (address and description of property) . . . .

. . . .

let under a lease dated . . . . and made between . . . .

. . . .

. . . .

of which you are the tenant.

3. I/we [propose to transfer] [transferred on ....][1] the whole of the landlord's interest and wish to be released from the landlord's obligations under the tenancy with effect from the date of the transfer. *[see Note 2 overleaf]*

4. If you consider that it is reasonable for me/us to be released, you do not need to do anything, but it would help me/us if you notify me/us using Part II of this Form. *[see Note 3 overleaf]*

5. If you do not consider it reasonable for me/us to be released, you must notify me/us of your objection, using Part II of this Form, within the period of **FOUR WEEKS** beginning with the giving of this notice, or I/we will be released in any event. You may withdraw your objection at any time by notifying me/us in writing. *[see Notes 4–6 overleaf]*

---

1 Delete alternative as appropriate.

6. All correspondence about this notice should be sent to the landlord/landlord's agent at the address given below.

Date.............Signature of landlord/landlord's agent ....

Name and address of landlord.....................................

....

....

[Name and address of agent ....

....

....]

NOTES TO PART I

Release of landlord

1. The landlord is about to transfer his interest to a new landlord, or has just done so, and is applying to be released from the obligations of the landlord under your tenancy. You have a number of options: you may expressly agree to the landlord's being released; you may object to his being released (with the option of withdrawing your objection later); or you may do nothing, in which case the landlord will automatically be released, with effect from the date of the transfer, once four weeks have elapsed from the date of the giving of the notice. If you choose to oppose release, you must act within four weeks of the giving of the notice.

Validity of notice

2. The landlord must give this notice either before the transfer or within the period of four weeks beginning with the date of the transfer. If the notice has been given late, it is not valid. You should read Note 4 below concerning the date of the giving of the notice.

Agreeing to release

3. If you are content for the landlord to be released, you may notify him of this using Part II of this Form, and the landlord will then be released as from the date of the transfer. If you do this, you may not later change your mind and object.

Objecting to release

4. If you think that it is not reasonable for the landlord to be released, you may object to release by notifying the landlord, using Part II of this Form. You must, however, do this within four weeks of the date of the giving of the notice. The date of the giving of the notice may not be the date written on the notice or the date on which you actually saw it. It may, for instance, be the date on which the notice was delivered through the post to your last address known by the landlord. If there has been any delay in your seeing this notice you may need to act very quickly. If you are in any doubt, you should seek advice immediately. If you change your mind after objecting, you may consent instead, at any time, by notifying the landlord *in writing* that you now consent to his being released and that your objection is withdrawn.

5. If you object within the time limit, the landlord will only be released if *either* he applies to a court and the court decides that it is reasonable for him to be released, *or* you withdraw your objection by a notice in writing as explained in Note 4 above.

6. In deciding whether to object, you should bear in mind that if the court finds that it is reasonable for the landlord to be released, or if you withdraw your objection late, you may have to pay costs.

PART II

TENANT'S RESPONSE TO LANDLORD'S NOTICE APPLYING FOR RELEASE FROM LANDLORD COVENANTS OF A TENANCY ON ASSIGNMENT OF WHOLE OF REVERSION
(Landlord and Tenant (Covenants) Act 1995, Section 8)

To [name and address]: . . . .

. . . .

1. This notice is given under Section 8 of the Landlord and Tenant (Covenants) Act 1995.

2. It relates to (address and description of property) . . . .

. . . .

let under a lease dated . . . . and made between . . . .

. . . .

. . . .

of which you are the landlord or have just transferred the landlord's interest.

3. You [propose to transfer] [transferred on ....][1] the landlord's interest and have applied to be released from the landlord's obligations under the tenancy with effect from the date of the transfer.

4.[2] I/we agree to your being released from the landlord's obligations with effect from the date of the transfer. *{see Note 1 overleaf}*

OR

4. I/we do not consider it reasonable that you should be released from the landlord's obligations, and object to the release. *{see Notes 2 and 3 overleaf}*

5. All correspondence about this notice should be sent to the tenant/tenant's agent at the address given below.

Date . . . . Signature of tenant/tenant's agent . . . .

Name and address of tenant . . . .

. . . .

. . . .

[Name and address of agent . . . .

. . . .

. . . .]

---

1 Delete alternative as appropriate.

2 The tenant should select one version of paragraph 4 and cross out the other.

NOTES TO PART II

Agreement to release

1. If the tenant has indicated agreement in paragraph 4 of the notice, you will automatically be released from the landlord' s obligations under the tenancy with effect from the date of your transfer of the landlord's interest.

Objection to release

2. If the tenant has indicated an objection in paragraph 4 of the notice, you will not be released unless either the tenant later withdraws his objection or you apply to the County Court to declare that it is reasonable for you to be released, and the court so declares. If you are not released, you may still apply for release when the landlord's interest, or part of it, is next transferred, and it may therefore be sensible to make arrangements for the person to whom you are making the transfer to inform you when he intends to transfer the landlord's interest in his turn.

Validity of notice of objection

3. A notice of objection by the tenant is only valid if he has given it to you within the period of four weeks beginning with the date on which you gave him your notice applying for release. If you are in any doubt, you should seek advice before applying to the court.

FORM 4

PART I

LANDLORD'S NOTICE APPLYING FOR RELEASE FROM LANDLORD COVENANTS OF A TENANCY ON ASSIGNMENT OF PART OF REVERSION
(Landlord and Tenant (Covenants) Act 1995, Sections 6 and 8)

To [name and address]: ....

. . . .

IMPORTANT – THE PERSON GIVING THIS NOTICE IS PROTECTING THE RIGHT TO RECOVER THE AMOUNT(S) SPECIFIED FROM YOU NOW OR AT SOME TIME IN THE FUTURE. THERE MAY BE ACTION WHICH YOU CAN TAKE TO PROTECT YOUR POSITION. READ THE NOTICE AND ALL THE NOTES OVERLEAF CAREFULLY. IF YOU ARE IN ANY DOUBT ABOUT THE ACTION YOU SHOULD TAKE, SEEK ADVICE IMMEDIATELY, FOR INSTANCE FROM A SOLICITOR OR CITIZENS' ADVICE BUREAU.

---

1. This notice is given under Section 8 of the Landlord and Tenant (Covenants) Act 1995. *{see Note 1 overleaf}*

2. It relates to (address and description of property) ....

. . . .

let under a lease dated .... and made between ....

. . . .

. . . .

of which you are the tenant.

3. I/We [propose to transfer] [transferred on ....]¹ part of the landlord's interest, namely

. . . .

and wish to be released from the landlord's obligations under the tenancy, to the extent that they fall to be complied with in relation to that part, with effect from the date of the transfer. *{see Note 2 overleaf}*

4. If you consider that it is reasonable for me/us to be released, you do not need to do anything, but it would help me/us if you notify me/us using Part II of this Form. [see Note 3 overleaf]. *{see Note 3 overleaf}*

5. If you do **not** consider it reasonable for me/us to be released, you **must** notify me/us of your objection, using Part II of this Form, within the period of **FOUR WEEKS** beginning with the giving of this notice, or I/we will be released in any event. You may withdraw your objection at any time by notifying me/us in writing. *{see Notes 4–6 overleaf}*

---

1 Delete alternative as appropriate.

6. All correspondence about this notice should be sent to the landlord/landlord's agent at the address given below.

Date............. Signature of landlord/landlord's agent ....

Name and address of landlord..

....

....

[Name and address of agent ....

....

....]

NOTES TO PART I

Release of landlord

1. The landlord is about to transfer part of his interest to a new landlord, or has just done so, and is applying to be released from the obligations of the landlord under your tenancy, to the extent that they fall to be complied with in relation to that part. You have a number of options: you may expressly agree to the landlord's being released; you may object to his being released (with the option of withdrawing your objection later); or you may do nothing, in which case the landlord will automatically be released, with effect from the date of the assignment, once four weeks have elapsed from the date of the giving of the notice. If you choose to oppose release, you must act within four weeks of the giving of the notice.

Validity of notice

2. The landlord must give this notice either before the transfer or within the period of four weeks beginning with the date of the transfer. If the notice has been given late, it is not valid. You should read Note 4 below concerning the date of the giving of the notice.

Agreeing to release

3. If you are content for the landlord to be released, you may notify him of this using Part II of this Form, and the landlord will then be released as from the date of the transfer. If you do this, you may not later change your mind and object.

Objecting to release

4. If you think that it is not reasonable for the landlord to be released, you may object to release by notifying the landlord, using Part II of this Form. You must, however, do this within four weeks of the date of the giving of the notice. The date of the giving of the notice may not be the date written on the notice or the date on which you actually saw it. It may, for instance, be the date on which the notice was delivered through the post to your last address known to the person giving the notice. If there has been any delay in your seeing this notice you may need to act very quickly. If you are in any doubt, you should seek advice immediately. If you change your mind after objecting, you may consent instead, at any time, by notifying the landlord in writing that you now consent

to his being released and that your objection is withdrawn.

5. If you object within the time limit, the landlord will only be released if either he applies to a court and the court decides that it is reasonable for him to be released, or you withdraw your objection by a notice in writing as explained in Note 4 above.

6. In deciding whether to object, you should bear in mind that if the court finds that it is reasonable for the landlord to be released, or if you withdraw your objection late, you may have to pay costs.

PART II

TENANT'S RESPONSE TO LANDLORD'S NOTICE APPLYING FOR RELEASE FROM LANDLORD COVENANTS OF A TENANCY ON ASSIGNMENT OF PART OF REVERSION
(Landlord and Tenant (Covenants) Act 1995, Section 8)

To [name and address]:. . . . .

. . . .

1. This notice is given under Section 8 of the Landlord and Tenant (Covenants) Act 1995.

2. It relates to (address and description of property) . . . .

. . . .

let under a lease dated . . . . and made between . . . .

. . . .

. . . .

of which you are the landlord or have just transferred part of the landlord's interest.

3. You [propose to transfer] [transferred on ....][1] part of the landlord's interest, namely

. . . .

and have applied to be released from the landlord's obligations under the tenancy, to the extent that they fall to be complied with in relation to that part, with effect from the date of the transfer.

4.[2] I/we agree to your being released from the landlord's obligations to that extent with effect from the date of the transfer. *[see Note 1 overleaf]*

OR

4. I/we do not consider it reasonable that you should be released from the landlord's obligations, and object to the release. *[see Notes 2 and 3 overleaf]*

5. All correspondence about this notice should be sent to the tenant/tenant's agent at the address given below.

Date. . . . . Signature of tenant/tenant's agent . . . .

Name and address of tenant . . . .

. . . .

. . . .

[Name and address of agent . . . .

. . . .

. . . .]

---

1 Delete alternative as appropriate.

2 The tenant should select one version of paragraph 4 and cross out the other.

NOTES TO PART II

Agreement to release

1. If the tenant has indicated agreement in paragraph 4 of the notice, you will automatically be released from the landlord' s obligations under the tenancy, to the extent that they fall to be complied with in relation to the part of your interest being transferred, with effect from the date of the transfer.

Objection to release

2. If the tenant has indicated an objection in paragraph 4 of the notice, you will not be released unless either the tenant later withdraws his objection or you apply to the County Court to declare that it is reasonable for you to be released, and the court so declares. If you are not released, you may still apply for release when the landlord' s interest, or part of it, is next transferred, and it may therefore be sensible to make arrangements for the person to whom you are making the transfer to inform you when he intends to transfer the landlord's interest in his turn.

Validity of notice of objection

3. A notice of objection by the tenant is only valid if he has given it to you within the period of four weeks beginning with the date on which you gave him your notice applying for release. If you are in any doubt, you should seek advice before applying to the court.

FORM 5

PART I

FORMER LANDLORD'S NOTICE APPLYING FOR RELEASE FROM LANDLORD COVENANTS OF A TENANCY
(Landlord and Tenant (Covenants) Act 1995, Sections 7 and 8)

To [name and address]: . . . .

. . . .

> IMPORTANT – THE PERSON GIVING THIS NOTICE IS PROTECTING THE RIGHT TO RECOVER THE AMOUNT(S) SPECIFIED FROM YOU NOW OR AT SOME TIME IN THE FUTURE. THERE MAY BE ACTION WHICH YOU CAN TAKE TO PROTECT YOUR POSITION. READ THE NOTICE AND ALL THE NOTES OVERLEAF CAREFULLY. IF YOU ARE IN ANY DOUBT ABOUT THE ACTION YOU SHOULD TAKE, SEEK ADVICE IMMEDIATELY, FOR INSTANCE FROM A SOLICITOR OR CITIZENS' ADVICE BUREAU.

1. This notice is given under Section 8 of the Landlord and Tenant (Covenants) Act 1995. *{see Note 1 overleaf}*

2. It relates to (address and description of property) . . . .

. . . .

let under a lease dated . . . . and made between . . . .

. . . .

. . . .

of which you are the tenant.

3. I/we was/were formerly landlord of the property of which you are tenant and remained bound by the landlord's obligations under the tenancy after transferring the landlord's interest. The landlord's interest, or part of it [is about to be transferred] [was transferred on . . . .][1]. I/we wish to be released from my/our obligations with effect from the date of that transfer. *{see Note 2 overleaf}*

4. If you consider that it is reasonable for me/us to be released, you do not need to do anything, but it would help me/us if you notify me/us using Part II of this Form. *{see Note 3 overleaf}*

5. If you do **not** consider it reasonable for me/us to be released, you must notify me/us of your objection, using Part II of this Form, within the period of **FOUR WEEKS** beginning with the giving of this notice, or I/we will be released in any event. You may withdraw your objection at any time by notifying me/us in writing. *{see Notes 4–6 overleaf}*

6. All correspondence about this notice should be sent to the former landlord/former landlord' s agent at the address given below.

---

1 Delete alternative as appropriate.

Date. . . . . Signature of former landlord/agent. . . . .

Name and address of former landlord. . . . .

. . . .

. . . .

[Name and address of agent . . . .

. . . .

. . . .]

NOTES TO PART I

Release of former landlord

1. Your landlord is about to transfer his interest, or part of it, to a new landlord, or has just done so, and a former landlord of the property is applying to be released from his obligations, from which he was not released when he transferred the landlord's interest himself. You have a number of options: you may expressly agree to the former landlord's being released; you may object to his being released (with the option of withdrawing your objection later); or you may do nothing, in which case the former landlord will automatically be released, with effect from the date of the present transfer, once four weeks have elapsed from the date of the giving of the notice. If you choose to oppose release, you must act within four weeks of the giving of the notice.

Validity of notice

2. The former landlord is required to give this notice either before the transfer by the present landlord takes place or within the period of four weeks beginning with the date of the transfer. If the notice has been given late, it is not valid. You should read Note 4 below concerning the date of the giving of the notice.

Agreeing to release

3. If you are content for the former landlord to be released, you may notify him of this using Part II of this Form, and the former landlord will then automatically be released as from the date of the present transfer. If you do this, you may not later change your mind and object.

Objecting to release

4. If you think that it is not reasonable for the former landlord to be released, you may object to release by notifying the former landlord, using Part II of this Form. You must, however, do this within four weeks of the date of the giving of the notice. The date of the giving of the notice may not be the date written on the notice or the date on which you actually saw it. It may, for instance, be the date on which the notice was delivered through the post to your last address known to the person giving the notice. If there has been any delay in your seeing this notice you may need to act very quickly. If you are in any doubt, you should seek advice immediately. If you change your mind after objecting, you may consent instead, at any time, by notifying the former landlord in writing that you now consent to his being released and that your objection is withdrawn.

5. If you object within the time limit, the former landlord will only be released if either he applies to a court and the court decides that it is reasonable for him to be released, or you withdraw your objection by a notice in writing as explained in Note 4 above.

6. In deciding whether to object, you should bear in mind that if the court finds that it is reasonable for the former landlord to be released, or if you withdraw your objection late, you may have to pay costs.

PART II

TENANT'S RESPONSE TO FORMER LANDLORD'S NOTICE APPLYING FOR RELEASE FROM LANDLORD COVENANTS OF A TENANCY
(Landlord and Tenant (Covenants) Act 1995, Section 8)

To [name and address]: . . . .

. . . .

1. This notice is given under Section 8 of the Landlord and Tenant (Covenants) Act 1995.

2. It relates to (address and description of property) . . . .

. . . .

let under a lease dated . . . . and made between . . . .

. . . .

. . . .

of which you were formerly landlord.

3. You have applied to be released from the landlord's obligations under the tenancy with effect from the date of a [proposed transfer] [transfer on ....][1] of the landlord's interest.

4.[2] I/we agree to your being released from the landlord's obligations with effect from the date of that transfer. *{see Note I overleaf}*

OR

4. I/we do not consider it reasonable that you should be released from the landlord's obligations, and object to your being so released. *{see Notes 2 and 3 overleaf}*

5. All correspondence about this notice should be sent to the tenant/tenant's agent at the address given below.

Date . . . . Signature of tenant/tenant's agent . . . .

Name and address of tenant . . . .

. . . .

. . . .

[Name and address of agent . . . .

. . . .

. . . .]

---

1 Delete alternative as appropriate.

2 The tenant should select one version of paragraph 4 and cross out the other.

NOTES TO PART II

Agreement to release

1. If the tenant has indicated agreement in paragraph 4 of the notice, you will automatically be released from the landlord's obligations under the tenancy with effect from the date of the transfer by the present landlord.

Objection to release

2. If the tenant has indicated an objection in paragraph 4 of the notice, you will not be released unless *either* the tenant later withdraws his objection *or* you apply to the County Court to declare that it is reasonable for you to be released, and the court so declares. If you are not released, you may still apply for release when the reversion, or part of it, is next assigned, and it may therefore be sensible to make arrangements for you to be informed when the present landlord's transferee intends to transfer the landlord's interest in his turn.

Validity of notice of objection

3. A notice of objection by the tenant is only valid if he has given it to you within the period of four weeks beginning with the date on which you gave him your notice applying for release. If you are in any doubt, you should seek advice before applying to the court.

FORM 6

PART I

FORMER LANDLORD'S NOTICE APPLYING FOR RELEASE FROM LANDLORD COVENANTS OF A TENANCY (FORMER LANDLORD HAVING ASSIGNED PART OF REVERSION)
(Landlord and Tenant (Covenants) Act 1995, Sections 7 and 8)

To [name and address]: . . . .

. . . .

> IMPORTANT – THE PERSON GIVING THIS NOTICE IS PROTECTING THE RIGHT TO RECOVER THE AMOUNT(S) SPECIFIED FROM YOU NOW OR AT SOME TIME IN THE FUTURE. THERE MAY BE ACTION WHICH YOU CAN TAKE TO PROTECT YOUR POSITION. READ THE NOTICE AND ALL THE NOTES OVERLEAF CAREFULLY. IF YOU ARE IN ANY DOUBT ABOUT THE ACTION YOU SHOULD TAKE, SEEK ADVICE IMMEDIATELY, FOR INSTANCE FROM A SOLICITOR OR CITIZENS' ADVICE BUREAU.

1. This notice is given under Section 8 of the Landlord and Tenant (Covenants) Act 1995. *{see Note 1 overleaf}*

2. It relates to (address and description of property) . . . .

. . . .

let under a lease dated . . . . and made between . . . .

. . . .

. . . .

of which you are the tenant.

3. I/we was/were formerly landlord of the property of which you are tenant and remained bound by all the landlord's obligations under the tenancy after transferring part of the landlord's interest, namely

. . . .

The landlord's interest, or part of it [is about to be transferred] [was transferred on . . . .]¹. I/we wish to be released from my/our obligations with effect from the date of that transfer. *{see Note 2 overleaf}*

4. If you consider that it is reasonable for me/us to be released, you do not need to do anything, but it would help me/us if you notify me/us using Part II of this Form. *{see Note 3 overleaf}*

5. If you do **not** consider it reasonable for me/us to be released, you must notify me/us of your objection, using Part II of this Form, within the period of **FOUR WEEKS** beginning with the giving of this notice, or I/we will be released in any event. You may

---

1 Delete as appropriate.

withdraw your objection at any time by notifying me/us in writing. *[see Notes 4–6 below]*

6. All correspondence about this notice should be sent to the former landlord/former landlord's agent at the address given below.

Date............Signature of former landlord/agent....................

Name and address of former landlord................................

....

....

[Name and address of agent ....

....

....]

NOTES TO PART I

Release of former landlord

1. Your landlord is about to transfer his interest, or part of it, to a new landlord, or has just done so, and a former landlord of the property is applying to be released from his obligations in relation to part of the landlord's interest, from which he was not released when he transferred that part himself. You have a number of options: you may expressly agree to the former landlord's being released; you may object to his being released (with the option of withdrawing your objection later); or you may do nothing, in which case the former landlord will automatically be released, with effect from the date of the present transfer, once four weeks have elapsed from the date of the giving of the notice. If you choose to oppose release, you must act within four weeks of the giving of the notice.

Validity of notice

2. The former landlord is required to give this notice either before the transfer by the present landlord takes place or within the period of four weeks beginning with the date of the transfer. If the notice has been given late, it is not valid. You should read Note 4 below concerning the date of the giving of the notice.

Agreeing to release

3. If you are content for the former landlord to be released, you may notify him of this using Part II of this Form, and the former landlord will then automatically be released as from the date of the present transfer. If you do this, you may not later change your mind and object.

Objecting to release

4. If you think that it is not reasonable for the former landlord to be released, you may object to release by notifying the former landlord, using Part II of this Form. You must, however, do this within four weeks of the date of the giving of the notice. The date of the giving of the notice may not be the date written on the notice or the date on which you actually saw it. It may, for instance, be the date on which the notice was delivered

through the post to your last address known to the person giving the notice. If there has been any delay in your seeing this notice you may need to act very quickly. If you are in any doubt, you should seek advice immediately. If you change your mind after objecting, you may consent instead, at any time, by notifying the former landlord in writing that you now consent to his being released and that your objection is withdrawn.

5. If you object within the time limit, the former landlord will only be released if either he applies to a court and the court decides that it is reasonable for him to be released, or you withdraw your objection by a notice in writing as explained in Note 4 above.

6. In deciding whether to object, you should bear in mind that if the court finds that it is reasonable for the former landlord to be released, or if you withdraw your objection late, you may have to pay costs.

PART II

TENANT'S RESPONSE TO FORMER LANDLORD'S NOTICE APPLYING FOR RELEASE FROM LANDLORD COVENANTS OF A TENANCY (FORMER LANDLORD HAVING ASSIGNED PART OF REVERSION)
(Landlord and Tenant (Covenants) Act 1995, Section 8)

To [name and address]: ....

....

1. This notice is given under Section 8 of the Landlord and Tenant (Covenants) Act 1995.

2. It relates to (address and description of property) ....

....

let under a lease dated . . . . and made between . . . .

....

....

of which you were formerly landlord.

3. You remain bound by the landlord's obligations under the tenancy in relation to a part of the landlord's interest which you previously assigned, namely

....

You have applied to be released from those obligations, to the extent that they relate to that part, with effect from the date of a [proposed transfer] [transfer on . . . .]¹ of the landlord's interest.

4.² I/we agree to your being released from the landlord's obligations to that effect from the date of that transfer. *[see Note I overleaf]*

OR

4. I/we do not consider it reasonable that you should be released from the landlord's obligations, and object to your being so released. *[see Notes 2 and 3 overleaf]*

5. All correspondence about this notice should be sent to the tenant/tenant's agent at the address given below.

Date . . . . Signature of tenant/tenant's agent . . . .

Name and address of tenant . . . .

....

....

[Name and address of agent . . . .

....

. . . .]

---

1 Delete alternative as appropriate.

2 The tenant should select one version of paragraph 4 and cross out the other.

NOTES TO PART II

Agreement to release

1. If the tenant has indicated agreement in paragraph 4 of the notice, you will automatically be released from the landlord's obligations under the tenancy to the appropriate extent with effect from the date of the transfer by the present landlord.

Objection to release

2. If the tenant has indicated an objection in paragraph 4 of the notice, you will not be released unless either the tenant later withdraws his objection or you apply to the County Court to declare that it is reasonable for you to be released, and the court so declares. If you are not released, you may still apply for release when the reversion, or part of it, is next transferred, and it may therefore be sensible to make arrangements for you to be informed when the present landlord's transferee intends to transfer the landlord's interest in his turn.

Validity of notice of objection

3. A notice of objection by the tenant is only valid if he has given it to you within the period of four weeks beginning with the date on which you gave him your notice applying for release. If you are in any doubt, you should seek advice before applying to the court.

FORM 7

PART I

JOINT NOTICE BY TENANT AND ASSIGNEE FOR BINDING APPORTIONMENT OF LIABILITY UNDER NON-ATTRIBUTABLE TENANT COVENANTS OF A TENANCY ON ASSIGNMENT OF PART OF PROPERTY
(Landlord and Tenant (Covenants) Act 1995, Sections 9 and 10)

To [name and address]: . . . .

. . . .

IMPORTANT – THE PERSON GIVING THIS NOTICE IS PROTECTING THE RIGHT TO RECOVER THE AMOUNT(S) SPECIFIED FROM YOU NOW OR AT SOME TIME IN THE FUTURE. THERE MAY BE ACTION WHICH YOU CAN TAKE TO PROTECT YOUR POSITION. READ THE NOTICE AND ALL THE NOTES OVERLEAF CAREFULLY. IF YOU ARE IN ANY DOUBT ABOUT THE ACTION YOU SHOULD TAKE, SEEK ADVICE IMMEDIATELY, FOR INSTANCE FROM A SOLICITOR OR CITIZENS' ADVICE BUREAU.

1. This notice is given under Section 8 of the Landlord and Tenant (Covenants) Act 1995. *{see Note 1 overleaf}*

2. It relates to (address and description of property) . . . .

. . . .

let under a lease dated . . . . and made between . . . .

. . . .

. . . .

of which you are the landlord.[1]

3. We are the parties to a [proposed transfer] [transfer on . . . .][2] of part of the property comprised in the tenancy, namely

. . . .

We are jointly and severally liable to perform the obligation(s) specified in the attached Schedule and have agreed to divide that liability between us in the manner specified in the Schedule.[3] We wish this agreement to be binding on you as well as between us, with effect from the date of the transfer. *{see Note 2 overleaf}*

---

1 'Landlord', for these purposes, includes any person for the time being entitled to enforce the obligations in question (for example, a management company).

2 Delete alternative as appropriate.

3 The Schedule must be in writing, and must specify the nature of the obligation, the term or condition of the Lease or other instrument under which it arises and the manner in which liability to perform it is divided under the agreement (for example, an obligation to pay service charge under a specific provision of the lease might be divided equally). It may be helpful to attach a copy of the agreement to the notice.

4. If you consider that it is reasonable for you to be bound by this agreement, you do not need to do anything, but it would help us if you notify us using Part II of this Form. *{see Note 3 overleaf}*

5. If you do **not** consider it reasonable for you to be bound by this agreement, you must notify both of us of your objection, using Part II of this Form, within the period of **FOUR WEEKS** beginning with the giving of this notice. You may withdraw your objection at any time by notifying us in writing. *{see Notes 4–6 overleaf}*

6. All correspondence about this notice should be copied, one copy sent to each of the parties to the agreement, at the addresses given below.

Signature of tenant/tenant's agent . . . .

Name and address of tenant . . . .

. . . .

. . . .

[Name and address of agent . . . .

. . . .

. . . .]

Signature of new tenant/agent . . . .

Name and address of new tenant . . . .

. . . .

. . . .

[Name and address of agent . . . .

. . . .

. . . .]

Date . . . .

NOTES TO PART I

Apportionment of liability

1. The tenant is about to transfer, or has just transferred, part of his interest to a new tenant, but they are jointly and severally liable for a particular obligation or obligations covering the whole of the property. They have agreed to divide that liability between them, and are applying for you as the landlord to be bound as well, so that you can only enforce the liability against each of them as set out in their agreement. If you are bound, any subsequent landlord to whom you may transfer your interest will also be bound. You have a number of options: you may expressly agree to be bound; you may object to being bound (with the option of withdrawing your objection later); or you may do nothing, in which case you will automatically be bound, with effect from the date of the transfer, once four weeks have elapsed from the date of the giving of the notice. If

you choose to object, you must act within four weeks of the giving of the notice.

Validity of notice

2. This notice must be given either before the transfer or within the period of four weeks beginning with the date of the transfer. If the notice has been given late, it is not valid. You should read Note 4 below concerning the date of the giving of the notice.

Agreeing to be bound

3. If you are content to be bound, you may notify the tenant and new tenant using Part II of this Form (sending a copy to each of them), and all of you will be bound with effect from the date of the transfer. If you do this, you may not later change your mind and object.

Objecting to being bound

4. If you think that it is not reasonable for you to be bound, you may object by notifying the tenant and new tenant, using Part II of this Form (sending a copy to each of them). You must, however, do this within four weeks of the date of the giving of this notice. The date of the giving of the notice may not be the date written on the notice or the date on which you actually saw it. It may, for instance, be the date on which the notice was delivered through the post to your last address known to the person giving the notice. If there has been any delay in your seeing this notice you may need to act very quickly. If you are in any doubt, you should seek advice immediately. If you change your mind after objecting, you may consent instead, at any time, by notifying both the tenant and new tenant in writing that you now consent to be bound and that your objection is withdrawn.

5. If you object within the time limit, the apportionment will only bind you if either the tenant and new tenant apply to a court and the court decides that it is reasonable for you to be bound, or you withdraw your objection by notice in writing as explained in Note 4 above.

6. In deciding whether to object, you should bear in mind that if the court finds that it is reasonable for you to be bound, or if you withdraw your objection late, you may have to pay costs.

PART II

LANDLORD'S RESPONSE TO JOINT NOTICE BY TENANT AND ASSIGNEE SEEKING BINDING APPORTIONMENT OF LIABILITY UNDER NON-ATTRIBUTABLE TENANT COVENANTS OF A TENANCY ON ASSIGNMENT OF PART OF PROPERTY
(Landlord and Tenant (Covenants) Act 1995, Section 10)

To [name and address]: ....

....

And [name and address]: ....

....

1. This notice is given under Section 10 of the Landlord and Tenant (Covenants) Act 1995.

2. It relates to (address and description of property) ....

....

let under a lease dated .... and made between ....

....

....

of which I/we am/are the landlord.[1]

3. You have applied for me/us to be bound by your agreement to divide liability between you with effect from the [proposed transfer] [transfer on ....][2] of part of the property comprised in the tenancy.

4.[3] I/we agree to be bound by your agreement with effect from the date of the transfer. *{see Note I overleaf}*

OR

4. I/we do not consider it reasonable that I/we should be bound by your agreement, and object to being so bound. *{see Notes 2 and 3 overleaf}*

6. All correspondence about this notice should be sent to the landlord/landlord's agent at the address given below.

Date............. Signature of landlord/landlord's agent ....

Name and address of landlord..

....

....

---

1 'Landlord', for these purposes, includes any person for the time being entitled to enforce the obligations in question (for example, a management company).

2 Delete alternative as appropriate.

3 The landlord should select one version of paragraph 4 and cross out the other.

[Name and address of agent ....

....

....]

NOTES TO PART II

Agreement to be bound

1. If the landlord has indicated agreement in paragraph 3 of the notice, he will automatically be bound by your agreement, with effect from the date of the transfer. Any subsequent landlord will also be bound.

Objection to being bound

2. If the landlord has indicated an objection in paragraph 3 of the notice, he will not be bound by your agreement unless *either* the landlord later withdraws his objection *or* you apply to the County Court to declare that it is reasonable for him to be bound, and the court so declares.

Validity of notice of objection

3. A notice of objection by the landlord is only valid if he has given it to each of you within the period of four weeks beginning with the date on which you gave him your notice applying for your agreement to become binding on him. If you are in any doubt, you should seek advice before applying to the court.

FORM 8

PART I

JOINT NOTICE BY LANDLORD AND ASSIGNEE FOR BINDING APPORTIONMENT OF LIABILITY UNDER NON-ATTRIBUTABLE LANDLORD COVENANTS OF A TENANCY ON ASSIGNMENT OF PART OF REVERSION
(Landlord and Tenant (Covenants) Act 1995, Sections 9 and 10)

To [name and address]: . . . .

. . . .

> IMPORTANT – THE PERSON GIVING THIS NOTICE IS PROTECTING THE RIGHT TO RECOVER THE AMOUNT(S) SPECIFIED FROM YOU NOW OR AT SOME TIME IN THE FUTURE. THERE MAY BE ACTION WHICH YOU CAN TAKE TO PROTECT YOUR POSITION. READ THE NOTICE AND ALL THE NOTES OVERLEAF CAREFULLY. IF YOU ARE IN ANY DOUBT ABOUT THE ACTION YOU SHOULD TAKE, SEEK ADVICE IMMEDIATELY, FOR INSTANCE FROM A SOLICITOR OR CITIZENS' ADVICE BUREAU.

1. This notice is given under Section 8 of the Landlord and Tenant (Covenants) Act 1995. *[see Note 1 overleaf]*

2. It relates to (address and description of property) . . . .

. . . .

let under a lease dated . . . . and made between . . . .

. . . .

. . . .

of which you are the tenant.

3. We are the parties to a [proposed transfer] [transfer on . . . .][1] of the landlord's interest in part of the property comprised in the tenancy, namely

. . . .

We are jointly and severally liable to perform the obligation(s) specified in the attached Schedule, and have agreed to divide that liability between us in the manner specified in the Schedule.2 We wish this agreement to be binding on you as well as between us, with effect from the date of the transfer. *[see Note 2 overleaf]*

4. If you consider that it is reasonable for you to be bound by this agreement, you do not need to do anything, but it would help us if you notify us using Part II of this Form. *[see Note 3 overleaf]*

---

1 Delete alternative as appropriate.

2 The Schedule must be in writing, and must specify the nature of the obligation, the term or condition of the Lease or other instrument under which it arises and the manner in which liability to perform it is divided under the agreement. It may be helpful to attach a copy of the agreement to the notice.

5. If you do **not** consider it reasonable for you to be bound by this agreement, you **must** notify both of us of your objection, using Part II of this Form, within the period of **FOUR WEEKS** beginning with the giving of this notice. You may withdraw your objection at any time by notifying us in writing. *[see Notes 4–6 overleaf]*

6. All correspondence about this notice should be copied, and one copy sent to each of the parties to the agreement, at the addresses given below.

Signature of landlord/landlord's agent . . . .

Name and address of landlord. . . . .

. . . .

. . . .

[Name and address of agent . . . .

. . . .

. . . .]

Signature of new landlord/agent . . . .

Name and address of landlord. . . . .

. . . .

. . . .

[Name and address of agent . . . .

. . . .

. . . .]

Date . . . .

NOTES TO PART I

Apportionment of liability

1. The landlord is about to transfer, or has just transferred, part of his interest to a new landlord, but they are jointly and severally liable for a particular obligation or obligations covering the whole of the property. They have agreed to divide that liability between them, and are applying for you as tenant to be bound as well, so that you can only enforce the liability against each of them as set out in their agreement. If you are bound, any subsequent tenant to whom you may transfer your interest will also be bound. You have a number of options: you may expressly agree to be bound; you may object to being bound (with the option of withdrawing your objection later); or you may do nothing, in which case you will automatically be bound, with effect from the date of the transfer, once four weeks have elapsed from the date of the giving of the notice. If you choose to object, you must act within four weeks of the giving of the notice.

Validity of notice

2. This notice must be given either before the transfer or within the period of four weeks

beginning with the date of the transfer. If the notice has been given late, it is not valid. You should read Note 4 below concerning the date of the giving of the notice.

Agreeing to be bound

3. If you are content to be bound, you may notify the landlord and new landlord using Part II of this Form (sending a copy to each of them), and all of you will be bound with effect from the date of the transfer. If you do this, you may not later change your mind and object.

Objecting to being bound

4. If you think that it is not reasonable for you to be bound, you may object by notifying the landlord and new landlord, using Part II of this Form (sending a copy to each of them). You must, however, do this within four weeks of the date of the giving of the notice. The date of the giving of the notice may not be the date written on the notice or the date on which you actually saw it. It may, for instance be the date on which the notice was delivered through the post to your last address known to the person giving the notice. If there has been any delay in your seeing this notice you may need to act very quickly. If you are in any doubt, you should seek advice immediately. If you change your mind after objecting, you may consent instead, at any time, by notifying *both* the landlord and new landlord in writing that you now consent to be bound and that your objection is withdrawn.

5. If you object within the time limit, the apportionment will only bind you if *either* the landlord and new landlord apply to a court and the court decides that it is reasonable for you to be bound, *or* you withdraw your objection by notice in writing as explained in Note 4 above.

6. In deciding whether to object, you should bear in mind that if the court finds that it is reasonable for you to be bound, *or* if you withdraw your objection late, you may have to pay costs.

PART II

TENANT'S RESPONSE TO JOINT NOTICE BY LANDLORD AND ASSIGNEE SEEKING BINDING APPORTIONMENT OF LIABILITY UNDER NON-ATTRIBUTABLE LANDLORD COVENANTS OF A TENANCY ON ASSIGNMENT OF PART OF REVERSION
(Landlord and Tenant (Covenants) Act 1995, Section 10)

To [name and address]: . . . .

. . . .

And [name and address]: . . . .

. . . .

1. This notice is given under Section 10 of the Landlord and Tenant (Covenants) Act 1995.

2. It relates to (address and description of property) . . . .

. . . .

let under a lease dated . . . . and made between . . . .

. . . .

. . . .

of which I/we am/are the tenant.

3. You have applied for me/us to be bound by your agreement to divide liability between you with effect from the [proposed transfer] [transfer on . . . .][1] of part of the landlord's interest in the property comprised in the tenancy.

4.[2] I/we agree to be bound by your agreement with effect from the date of the transfer. *{see Note I overleaf}*

OR

4. I/we do not consider it reasonable that I/we should be bound by your agreement, and object to being so bound. *{see Notes 2 and 3 overleaf}*

6. All correspondence about this notice should be sent to the tenant/tenant's agent at the address given below.

Date . . . . Signature of tenant/tenant's agent . . . .

Name and address of tenant . . . .

. . . .

. . . .

---

1 Delete alternative as appropriate.

2 The tenant should select one version of paragraph 4 and cross out the other.

[Name and address of agent ....

....

....]

NOTES TO PART II

Agreement to be bound

1. If the tenant has indicated agreement in paragraph 3 of the notice, he will automatically be bound by your agreement, with effect from the date of the transfer. Any subsequent tenant will also be bound.

Objection to being bound

2. If the tenant has indicated an objection in paragraph 3 of the notice, he will not be bound by your agreement unless *either* the tenant later withdraws his objection *or* you apply to the County Court to declare that it is reasonable for him to be bound, and the court so declares.

Validity of notice of objection

3. A notice of objection by the tenant is only valid if he has given it to each of you within the period of four weeks beginning with the date on which you gave him your notice applying for your agreement to become binding on him. If you are in any doubt, you should seek advice before applying to the court.

EXPLANATORY NOTE

(This note is not part of the Regulations)

These Regulations prescribe the forms of notices to be used for the purposes of the Landlord and Tenant (Covenants) Act 1995. The forms are to be used for:

— notification by a landlord to a former tenant or guarantor who remains liable in respect of a covenant of the tenancy to pay a fixed charge, that sums for which he is liable under that covenant have become due and remain unpaid, and that the landlord intends to recover them from that person (Form I);

— further notification by a landlord to a former tenant or guarantor, that a sum payable in respect of a fixed charge of which he has been given notice has now been determined to be greater than specified in the original notice, and that the landlord intends to recover that greater sum from that person (Form 2);

— a landlord's application for release from the covenants in the tenancy on assignment of his interest and for the tenant's response to this application (Form 3);

— a landlord's application for release from the covenants in the tenancy to the appropriate extent on assignment of part of his interest and for the tenant's response to this application (Form 4);

— a former landlord's application for release from the covenants in the tenancy on a subsequent assignment of the landlord's interest or part of it and for the tenant's response to this application (Form 5);

— a former landlord's application for release from the covenants in the tenancy to the appropriate extent on a subsequent assignment of the landlord's interest or part of it, where the former landlord assigned only part of the reversion, and for the tenant's response to this application (Form 6);

— an application by a tenant who assigns only part of his interest and the assignee to make an apportionment of their liability under certain covenants of the tenancy binding on the other party to the tenancy, and for the other party's response to this application (Form 7);

— an application by a landlord who assigns only part of his interest and the assignee to make an apportionment of their liability under certain covenants of the tenancy binding on the other party to the tenancy, and for the other party's response to this application (Form 8).

Reproductions or facsimiles of the notices may be used provided that they are substantially in the same form as prescribed in the Schedule to the regulations, including the notes.

STATUTORY INSTRUMENTS

1995 No. 3153

LANDLORD AND TENANT, ENGLAND AND WALES

The Land Registration (No. 3) Rules 1995

Made	*6th December 1995*
Laid before Parliament	*6th December 1995*
Coming into force	*1st January 1996*

The Lord Chancellor with the advice and assistance of the Rule Committee appointed in pursuance of Section 144 of the Land Registration Act 1925(**a**), in exercise of the powers conferred on him by that section and by Section 38(2) of that Act(**b**) hereby makes the following rules:

PART I

GENERAL

Citation commencement and interpretation

1.—(1) These rules may be cited as the Land Registration (No 3) Rules 1995 and shall come into force on 1 January 1996.

(2) In these rules:

   (a) the principal rules' means the Land Registration Rules 1925(**c**);

   (b) a rule referred to by number means the rule so numbered in the principal rules.

PART II

DEFINITION OF "PROPER OFFICE"

Amendment to rule 1

2. The following paragraph is substituted for paragraph. (5A) of rule 1:

'(5A) 'Proper office' for the purposes of any application means the district registry within whose district, as constituted by orders made from time to time under Section 132(1) of the Act, the land to which the application relates is situated or, where it is situated in the districts of two or more district registries, either or any of those district registries.'

(a) 1925 c 21; Section 144(1) was amended by the Administration of Justice Act 1982 (c 53), Section 67(2) and Schedule 5, paragraph (d). The reference to the Ministry of Agriculture, Fisheries and Food was substituted by the Transfer of Functions (Ministry of Food) Order 1955 (SI 1955/554).

(b) Amended by the Law of Property (Miscellaneous Provisions) Act 1994 (c 36), Section 2(1) and Schedule 1 para 2.

(c) S.R. & O. 1925/1093; relevant amending instruments SI 1990/3275 and 1995/377.

Revocation of rules 24(4) and 83(2)

3. Rules 24(4)(**a**) and 83(2)(**b**) are revoked.

Amendments to rules other than the principal rules

4.—(1) The definitions of 'proper office' in rule 1(2) of the Land Registration (Open Register) Rules 1991(**c**) and rule 2(1) of the Land Registration (Official Searches) Rules 1993(**d**) are revoked.

(2) The following is substituted for the definition of 'proper office' in rule 2(1) of the Land Registration (Matrimonial Homes) Rules 1990(**e**):

' "proper office" has the meaning given to it by rule 1(5A) of the Land Registration Rules 1925(**f**).'

PART III

REGISTERED DEALINGS WITH REGISTERED LAND

Amendment to rule 1

5. In rule 1 the following paragraphs are inserted after paragraph (5J):

'(5K) In these rules 'new tenancy' has the same meaning as in Section 1 of the Landlord and Tenant (Covenants) Act 1995(**g**), and 'old tenancy' means a lease which is not a new tenancy.

(5L) In these rules references to:

  (a) Section 24 of the Act; or

  (b) Section 77 of, or Schedule 2 to, the Law of Property Act 1925 as originally enacted,

are references to those provisions as they operate in relation to old tenancies by virtue of Section 30(3) of the Landlord and Tenant (Covenants) Act 1995.'

Revocation of rule 76

6. Rule 76 is revoked.

New rule 109

7.—(1) The following rule is substituted for rule 109:

'Transfer of land subject to a rentcharge

109.—(1) A transfer of land subject to a rentcharge not falling within paragraph (2) below shall be made by an instrument in Form 19 or 32.

(2) A transfer of part of land subject to a rentcharge in which the rent is apportioned or land is exonerated from it shall be made by an instrument in Form 34B, or as near thereto as circumstances permit.

(3) Where the covenants set out in Part VII or Part VIII of Schedule 2 to the Law of Property Act 1925(**h**) (in this rule called 'the 1925 Act') are included in a transfer,

---

(**a**) Added by SI 1990/314, rule 7.	(**b**) Inserted by SI 1990/314, rule 9.
(**c**) SI 1992/122	(**d**) SI 1993/3276.
(**e**) 1990/1360.	(**f**) S.R. & O. 1925/1093.
(**g**) 1995 c 30.	(**h**) 15 Geo. 5 c 20.

the references to 'the grantees', 'the conveyance' and 'the conveying parties' shall be treated as references to the transferees, the transfer and the transferors respectively.

(4) Where in a transfer part of land affected by a rentcharge is, without the consent of the owner of the rentcharge, expressed to be transferred exonerated from the entire rent, and the covenants in paragraph (ii) of Part VIII of Schedule 2 to the 1925 Act are included, that paragraph shall apply as if:

(a) any reference to the balance of the rent were to the entire rent; and

(b) the words 'other than the covenant to pay the entire rent,' were omitted.

(5) Where in a transfer to which Section 77(1)(B) of the 1925 Act does not apply part of land affected by a rentcharge is, without the consent of the owner of the rentcharge, expressed to be transferred subject to or charged with the entire rent. and the covenants in paragraph (i) of Part VIII of Schedule 2 to the 1925 Act are included, that paragraph shall apply as if:

(a) any reference to the apportioned rent were to the entire rent; and

(b) the words 'than the covenant to pay the entire rent,' were omitted.

(6) On a transfer of land subject to a rentcharge:

(a) any covenant implied by Section 77(1)(A) or (B)(i) of the 1925 Act may be modified or negatived; and

(b) any covenant included in the instrument of transfer may be modified,

by adding suitable words to the instrument.'

(2) In the heading of Form 19 in the Schedule to the principal rules a reference to Rules 98 and 109 is substituted for the reference to Rule 98.

(3) The following note shall be inserted in the notes to Form 19 in the Schedule to the principal rules:

'(4A) Where the transfer is subject to a rentcharge (other than a rentcharge created after 22nd July 1977 by virtue of Section 2(3)(a) or (b) of the Rentcharges Act 1977**(a)**) and no covenants are implied by Section 77(1) of the Law of Property Act 1925**(b)**, the appropriate covenants may be incorporated by adding the words 'The covenants set out in Part VII (or *if the rent has previously been apportioned without the consent of the owner of the rentcharge*, paragraph (i) of Part VIII) of Schedule 2 to the Law of Property Act 1925 shall be included in this transfer'.

New Rules 115 and 116

8. The following rule is substituted for Rule 115:

'Transfer of leasehold land

'115.—(1) A transfer of leasehold land not falling within Rule 116 shall be made by an instrument in Form 32 or 33.

(2) Where the transfer is a transfer of an old tenancy and covenants are to be implied under Section 77 of the Law of Property Act 1925 as originally enacted, express reference shall be made in the transfer to that Section.'

(a) 1977 c.30.

(b) 15 Geo 5 c 20.

9. The following rule is substituted for Rule 116:

'Transfer of leasehold land, the rent being apportioned or land exonerated

116.—(1) A transfer of part of leasehold land in which the rent is apportioned or land is exonerated from it shall be made by an instrument in Form 34 or 34A, or as near thereto as circumstances will permit.

(2) Where in a transfer part of land held under an old tenancy is, without the consent of the lessor, expressed to be transferred exonerated from the entire rent, and the covenants in paragraph (ii) of Part X of Schedule 2 to the Law of Property Act 1925 as originally enacted are included, that paragraph shall apply as if:

(a) any reference to the balance of the rent were to the entire rent; and

(b) the words, 'other than the covenant to pay the entire rent,' were omitted.

(3) Where in a transfer to which Section 77(1)(D) of the Law of Property Act 1925 as originally enacted does not apply part of land held under an old tenancy is, without the consent of the lessor, expressed to be transferred subject to or charged with the entire rent, and the covenants in paragraph (i) of Part X of Schedule 2 to the Law of Property Act 1925 as originally enacted are included, that paragraph shall apply as if:

(a) any reference to the apportioned rent were to the entire rent; and

(b) the words, 'other than the covenant to pay the entire rent,' were omitted.

(4) Where the transfer is a transfer of part of the land held under an old tenancy and covenants are to be implied under Section 24 of the Act, express reference shall be made in the transfer to that section.'

New Rule 117

10. The following rule is substituted for Rule 117:

'Variation of implied covenants in transfer of land held under old tenancy

117.—(1) Where in a transfer the covenants set out in Part IX or Part X of Schedule 2 to the Law of Property Act 1925 as originally enacted are included, the references to 'the assignees', 'the conveyance' and 'the conveying parties' shall be treated as references to the transferees, the transfer and the transferors respectively.

(2) On a transfer of land held under an old tenancy:

(a) any covenants implied by Section 24 of the Act or by Section 77(1)(c) or (D)(i) of the Law of Property Act 1925 as originally enacted may be modified or negatived; and

(b) any covenants included in the instrument of transfer may be modified,

by adding suitable words to the instrument, and a note shall be made in the register.'

New Forms 32, 33, 34, 34A and 34B

11. Forms 32, 33, 34, 34A and 34B in the Schedule to these rules shall be substituted for Forms 32, 33 and 34 in the Schedule to the principal rules.

Dated 6th December 1995   *Mackay of Clashfern*, C

THE SCHEDULE

FORM 32—*Transfer of leasehold land (whole or part). (Rules 109 and 115.)*

As Form 19 or Form 20, adding at the end 'for the residue of the term granted by the registered lease.'

Where it is intended to negative the covenants implied by Section 24 of the Act in relation to the transfer of an old tenancy, the following words may be added to the form:

'The covenant by the transferor (or transferee, or the covenants by the transferor and transferee) implied by Section 24 of the Act is (or are) not to be implied.'

FORM 33—*Transfer of leasehold land (whole) being part of the land originally comprised in the Lease where the rent has already been apportioned (Rule 115.)*

(*Date*.) In consideration of   pounds (£   ), I, AB, of etc, transfer to CD, of etc, the land comprised in the title above referred to for the residue of the term granted by the registered lease subject to the apportioned rent of £   being part of the rent of £   reserved by the registered lease.

Note.—Where it is intended to negative the covenant implied by Section 24 of the Act in relation to the transfer of an old tenancy, the following words may be added to the form:

'The covenant by the transferee implied by Section 24 of the Act is not to be implied.'

FORM 34—*Transfer of land held under a new tenancy (part), in which the rent is apportioned or land exonerated. (Rule 116.)*

(Heading as in Form 19)

(*Date*.) In consideration of   pounds (£   ), AB, of etc, transfer to C D, of etc, the land shown and edged with red on the accompanying plan, being part of the land comprised in the title above referred to for the residue of the term granted by the registered lease.

It is agreed that liability for the payment of [*where rent previously apportioned* the previously apportioned rent of £   being part of] the rent reserved by the registered lease is apportioned between the parties as follows:

£   (*or* The whole) shall be payable out of the land hereby transferred

The balance of £   (*or* The whole) shall be payable out of the residue of the land in the title(s) above referred to

If the whole rent is to he payable by one party, omit whichever of the above does not apply and add, and the residue of the land in the title(s) above referred to (or the land hereby transferred *as the case may be*) is exonerated from the said rent.

(To be executed as Form 19 by both parties)

FORM 34A—*Transfer of land held under an old tenancy (part), in which the rent is apportioned or land exonerated. (Rule 116.)*

As Form 34, adding if desired, where the rent is apportioned or land exonerated without the consent of the lessor, 'The covenants set out in paragraph (ii) of Part X of Schedule 2 to the Law of Property Act 1925 shall be included in this transfer.'

The covenants set out in paragraph (i) of the said Part X may, where no covenants are implied by Section 77(1)(D)(i) of the Law of Property Act 1925 as originally enacted, be incorporated by omitting the words 'paragraph (ii) of'.

Mutual charges in support of the covenants may be added if desired, and if added should be accompanied by application to register notice thereof.

Where the rent is apportioned or land exonerated with the consent of the lessor and no covenants are implied by Section 77(1)(c) of the Law of Property Act 1925 as originally enacted, the appropriate covenants may be incorporated by adding the words, 'The covenants set out in Part IX of Schedule 2 to the Law of Property Act 1925 shall be included in this transfer.'

FORM 34B—*Transfer of kind subject to a rentcharge (part), in which the rent is apportioned or land exonerated. (Rule 109.)*

(Heading as in Form 19)

(*Date.*) In consideration of pounds (£   ), AB, of etc, hereby transfers to C D, of etc, the land shown and edged with red on the accompanying plan, being part of the land comprised in the title above referred to.

It is agreed that liability for the payment of [*where rent previously apportioned* the previously apportioned rent of £   being part of] the yearly rentcharge of £
created by (*describe instrument*) to which the land transferred with other land is subject, is apportioned between the parties as follows:

£   (*or* The whole) shall be payable out of the land hereby transferred

The balance of   £ (*or* The whole) shall be payable out of the residue of the land in the title(s) above referred to

If the whole rent is to be payable by one party, omit whichever of the above does not apply and add, and the residue of the land in the title(s) above referred to (or the land hereby transferred as the case may be) is exonerated from the said rent.

If the rent is apportioned or land exonerated without the consent of the owner of the rentcharge add, if desired: The covenants set out in paragraph (ii) of Part VIII of Schedule 2 to the Law of Property Act 1925 shall be included in this transfer.

(To be executed as Form 19 by both parties)

Note.—The covenants set out in paragraph (i) of the said Part VIII may, where no covenants are implied by Section 77(1)(B)(i) of the Law of Property Act 1925, be included by omitting the words 'paragraph (ii) of'.

Mutual charges in support of the covenants may be added if desired, and if added should be accompanied by application to register notice thereof.

Where the rent is apportioned or land exonerated with the consent of the owner of the rentcharge and no covenants are implied by Section 77(1)(A) of the Law of Property Act 1925, the appropriate covenants may be incorporated by adding the words, 'The covenants set out in Part VII of Schedule 2 to the Law of Property Act 1925 shall be included in this transfer.'

EXPLANATORY NOTE

(This note does not form part of the Rules)

These Rules, which come into force on 1 January 1996, amend the Land Registration Rules 1925 ('the 1925 Rules'), the Land Registration (Matrimonial Homes) Rules 1990, the Land Registration (Open Register) Rules 1991 and the Land Registration (Official Searches) Rules 1993.

'Proper office' is defined in Rule 1(5A) of the 1925 Rules for the purposes of all four of these sets of rules. The proper office is the district registry within whose district the land, or any of the land, to which an application relates is situated.

New rules are substituted for Rules 115 and 116 of the 1925 Rules to provide for transfers of land held under 'new tenancies' within the meaning of the Landlord and Tenant (Covenants) Act 1995 (that is, leases granted on or after 1 January 1996 otherwise than in pursuance of an agreement entered into, an option granted or a court order made before that date) as well as transfers of land held under leases which are not new tenancies.

The covenants implied by Section 24 of the Land Registration Act 1925 and Section 77 of the Law of Property Act 1925 as originally enacted, both repealed in relation to new tenancies, can only apply to transfers of land held under leases which are not new tenancies. This is reflected in the new rules.

Rule 76 of the 1925 Rules, which provided for land subject to a rentcharge and leasehold land to be transferred as beneficial owner, etc so as to imply the covenants by the transferor implied by Section 77 of the Law of Property Act 1925, is revoked. New rules and forms allow the appropriate covenants to be incorporated in transfers without the transfer being made as beneficial owner.

New Rule 109 (Transfers of land subject to a rentcharge) adapts the wording of Parts VII and VIII of Schedule 2 to the Law of Property Act 1925 to the requirements of registered conveyancing. It applies to transfers of either freehold or leasehold land.

A new Rule 117 (Variation of implied covenants in transfer of land held under old tenancy) adapts the wording of Parts IX and X of Schedule 2 (saved in relation to leases which are not new tenancies) to the requirements of registered conveyancing, and provides for a note to be made on the register when the implied covenants are modified or negatived.

New Forms 32, 33, 34, 34A and 34B are substituted for Forms 32, 33 and 34 in the Schedule to the 1925 Rules.

STATUTORY INSTRUMENTS

1995 No. 3154

LANDLORD AND TENANT, ENGLAND AND WALES

The Land Registration (Overriding Leases) Rules 1995

Made	*6th December 1995*
Laid before Parliament	*6th December 1995*
Coming into force	*1st January 1996*

The Lord Chancellor, with the advice and assistance of the Rule Committee appointed in pursuance of Section 144 of the Land Registration Act 1925(**a**), in exercise of the powers conferred on him by that section and by Section 20(2) of the Landlord and Tenant (Covenants) Act 1995(**b**), hereby makes the following rules

Citation and commencement

1. These rules may be cited as the Land Registration (Overriding Leases) Rules 1995 and shall come into force on 1 January 1996

Statement to be inserted in an overriding lease

2. The statement required by Section 20(2) of the Landlord and Tenant (Covenants) Act 1995 to be inserted into an overriding lease granted under Section 19 of that Act shall in relation to a registrable lease be in the following form:

'This lease is granted under Section 19 of the Landlord and Tenant (Covenants) Act 1995 and is (or is not) a new tenancy for the purposes of Section 1 of that Act.'

Dated 6th December 1995   *Mackay of Clashfern*, C.

(**a**) 1925 c 21; Section 144(1) was amended by the Administration of Justice Act 1982 (c 53), Section 67(2) and Schedule 5, paragraph (d). The reference to the Ministry of Agriculture, Fisheries and Food was substituted by the Transfer of Functions (Ministry of Food) Order 1955 (SI 1955/554).

(**b**) 1995 c 30.

EXPLANATORY NOTE

(This note does not form part of the rules.)

These rules, which come into force on 1 January 1996, prescribe the statement required by Section 20(2) of the Landlord and Tenant (Covenants) Act 1995 to be inserted into an overriding lease granted under Section 19 of that Act.*
